When the news of the Hollandia-Aitape invasions reached the 2nd Area Forces and 18th Army head-quarters, Japanese generals and admirals were stunned. They had not prepared themselves for assaults on these New Guinea bases far up the coast, so they had offered little or no resistance. Moreover, the stalwart defenses completed at Wewak had gone for naught. Further, since the Allies controlled the skies as well as the sea lanes, the 50,000 troops of the 18th Army had been cut off and isolated by the American leap frog operations.

The Japanese were cornered—so it appeared . . . .

PACIFIC STRIKE

BY LAWRENCE CORTESI

ZEBRA BOOKS
KENSINGTON PUBLISHING CORP.

ZEBRA BOOKS

are published by

KENSINGTON PUBLISHING CORP.
475 Park Avenue South
New York, N.Y. 10016

The lines in the Pacific in March of 1944 just before the
Allied leapfrog into Hollandia and Aitape on 22 April 1944

Chapter One

By March of 1944, the Allies dominated the Solomons-Bismarck Archipelago areas of the South and Southwest Pacific. The Americans had cleansed the Japanese from the Solomon Islands, swept them out of eastern New Guinea, overwhelmed them in southern New Britain, and driven them out of the Admiralties. And finally, the Allies had effectively neutralized the big enemy stronghold at Rabaul. Gen. Douglas MacArthur, CinC of the Southwest Pacific Allied forces, now planned his first giant step back to the Philippines.

The nearest effective Japanese base in the Bismarck Archipelago was now at Wewak, at the extreme northwest corner of Australian New Guinea, and even this base had been badly decimated from U.S. 5th Air Force air attacks. But, MacArthur had frowned on invading Wewak head on. Instead, the Southwest Pacific CinC devised a daring plan. He proposed to make a long, 400-mile jump into Hollandia on Dutch New Guinea, bypassing and cutting off the strong Japanese base at Wewak in the process.

The occupation of Hollandia would open Japan's East Indies empire to Allied air and sea attacks and truly threaten Japan's lifeline from the Indies, where Japan obtained the bulk of her needed resources to wage war. MacArthur called the plan Operation Reckless, and perhaps the plan was just that—reckless. The Japanese response to such an invasion would be as vicious and violent as their response to the invasion of Guadalcanal nearly two years earlier. MacArthur's strategy could bring disaster to the Allies in the Pacific after 1½ years of steady progress.

On March 8, 1944, General MacArthur flew up to Momote Airdrome in the Admiralties from his SWPA headquarters in Brisbane, Australia. He drove at once to 6th Army Headquarters at Cape Cretin beyond Momote Drome to organize Operation Reckless. American GIs and airmen on the Admiralties expressed surprise to see the SWPA CinC himself this far from Australia. But, when these men saw other VIPs flying into Momote on this same 8 March, they guessed that MacArthur had come here to discuss another offensive in the SWPA. The CinC was apparently wasting no time in continuing his initiative.

In attendance at the Cape Cretin conference with the SWPA CinC were Gen. Walter Krueger, commander of the 6th Army; Gen. George Kenney, commander of the 5th Air

Force; Adm. Daniel Barbey, commander of the U.S. Naval TF 77; Gen. Robert Eichelberger, commander of the 1st Corps, and Gen. Charles Hall of the U.S. IX Corps. These officers had served MacArthur since the Papuan campaign and most recently in the capture of the Admiralties.

"Gentlemen," MacArthur began, studying the officers about him, "we've got the Japanese on the run. We've got them confused and we've got them off guard. Our land and air forces have never been stronger. So, this is the time to launch our most ambitious initiative in the Southwest Pacific since the war began. With the reduction of Rabaul and the occupation of the Admiralties, we're ready for a new move."

The officers only listened.

MacArthur turned to an aide who lowered a huge map of New Guinea. The SWPA CinC then continued. "I want you to look up here—Hollandia in Dutch New Guinea. It's nearly four hundred miles from our nearest base at Saidor and four hundred twenty-five air miles from our major all weather airbase at Nadzab above Lae Harbor on Huon Gulf. If we can take Hollandia, we'll have advanced further in this one jump than we did during the entire war. And most important, we can establish air and naval bases that will put the East Indies within range of heavy attacks."

He tapped the map before continuing. "The Japanese have done an excellent job of developing airfields at Hollandia and Wakde-Sarmi, so we'd only need minimum effort to make Hollandia the biggest airbase in the Southwest Pacific.''

"Are you suggesting, sir,'' General Hall said, "that we by-pass Wewak and all the other strong enemy bases along the New Guinea coast north of Saidor?''

"Yes.''

"But our G-two estimates that the Japanese have at least fifty thousand troops in the Wewak area, and they have active airdromes at But and Boram.''

"I must tell you, Doug,'' Kenney now spoke, "while our heavy bombers may be within range of Hollandia, our light bombers and fighter planes are not.''

"You'll have to do something about that, George,'' MacArthur grinned.

But Kenney was in no mood for humor. "Our reconnaissance reports show that the Japanese have built a huge airbase at Wakde-Sarmi, one hundred miles north of Hollandia, an airfield at Aitape, one hundred twenty-five miles to the south, and three dromes on Hollandia itself. The Japanese have obviously given up on the Bismarck Archipelago and they apparently intend to strengthen everything from Wewak northward. Hollandia is right in the middle of this new strength.''

"I'm aware of that,'' MacArthur told the 5th Air Force commander.

"Are we sure we can make a leap like that?'' General Eichelberger asked. "Do we have the means? Frankly, I expected our next move to be against Wewak.''

"That's what the Japanese expect, too," General MacArthur said. "So they'll never be looking for us to hit way up at Hollandia. They have limited combat troops in the area according to the G-two reports, no more than a regiment. The rest of the enemy forces are service and air maintenance personnel. With a few regimental combat teams we can take Hollandia without difficulty.''

"General," Kenney spoke again, "we simply cannot supply fighter planes to protect such a landing that far up the coast. And, since the enemy has turned Hollandia and Wakde-Sarmi into major airbases, they may have swarms of aircraft against any invasion forces. Fifth Air Force may not be in a position to intercept any heavy air resistance.''

MacArthur turned to Admiral Barbey of TF 77. "Dan?''

Admiral Barbey nodded and shuffled through some papers in front of him. "I've been in consultation with Admiral Halsey. He knows that land based fighters can't protect an amphibious force so far north of Nadzab. So we've come up with a solution. Halsey has agreed to release two fast carriers from TF Fifty-eight to protect the invasion forces. He'll allow us to keep the carriers for three days after L-day. Both carriers can accommodate one hundred fighter planes each, and that should give us plenty of aircraft to intercept any Japanese air interdiction from

11

the Wakde-Sarmi airfields."

"This plan involves more than Hollandia," MacArthur continued. He tapped the map again at another spot. "This is Aitape, about one hundred twenty-five miles southeast of Hollandia and eight miles northwest of Wewak. The forces for this operation will be split into a pair of amphibious units. Operation Reckless is the plan for the invasion and occupation of Hollandia. We've also drawn up a plan called Operation Persecution for the invasion and occupation of Aitape. The Japanese have been building three airfields at Aitape near Tadji Plantation. At least one of them is operational and our engineers can have this airstrip ready for fighters within forty-eight hours after the invasion."

"Admiral Halsey has also agreed to release a fleet of eight small CVE carriers from TF fifty eight, seven to cover the Aitape landings," Admiral Barbey said. "These jeep carriers have a total of two hundred fighter planes among them, and we can keep these CVE's for up to thirty days. That should give us adequate protection until Fifth Air Force can bring planes into Tadji to take over the job of air cover at Hollandia."

"There's a second bonus to occupying Aitape besides assured air cover," MacArthur said. "We'll be able to keep a strong flanking force south of Hollandia to stem any Japanese attempt to move up the coast from Wewak. In fact, we intend to land as many troops as necessary at Aitape to make certain the Japanese cannot overrun the area."

"I see," General Kenney said.

"Walt Krueger will now fill you in on the details for this operation," MacArthur gestured.

Krueger rose from his chair, nodded at the SWPA CinC, and then the 6th Army commander shuffled through some papers in front of him. "We intend to land at Hollandia and Aitape simultaneously on the morning of April 22, Bob Eichelberger's First Corps will assault Hollandia. Although there may be as many as five thousand enemy troops there, we don't think more than a few hundred of them are fighting men. We'll use about thirty-two thousand men of our own for this operation. Eichelberger will have all three RCT's of the Twenty-fourth Infantry Division and two RCT's of the Forty-first Division. He'll also have a regiment of service troops and one of combat engineers. We'll have the Sixth Infantry Division and the Five hundred second Parachute Regiment as reserves, and they can relieve the Forty-first and Twenty-fourth troops by L plus ten."

"We've been assured of ample transports to carry this huge force," Admiral Barbey said. "The seven regiments will sail on eight APA's, two AKA transports, three LSD's, fourteen APD's, thirty LCI's and twenty LST's. We'll also have four AKs to carry cargo and supplies. The entire Reckless amphibious force will be escorted by the two fast carriers along with a fleet of cruisers and destroyers."

"Where will these troops make the assault?" Eichelberger asked.

"The Twenty-fourth Division will land at Tanahmerah Bay," Krueger said, "and the two RCT's of the Forty-first Division will land at Humboldt Bay. Combat engineers will land with the first wave to open the trails towards Lake Sentani so we can occupy the Sentani and Cyclops Airdromes as soon as possible. That must be our first objective—to take the airfields."

"If we have enough air support, we can take those fields in a hurry," General Eichelberger said.

"I'll expect Fifth Air Force to hit those Hollandia defenses continually for two weeks before the invasion," MacArthur said.

Gen. George Kenney did not answer.

"Now," Krueger continued, moving his finger down the map to Aitape. "General Hall will lead the forces on Operation Persecution. He'll have the One sixty-third Regiment of the Forty-first Division to make the initial landings, with a regiment from the Thirty-second Division and the One twelfth Cavalry Regiment in reserve. The One sixty-third will land on these beaches near Korako, designated Blue Beach, about five miles southeast of Aitape village. A road from the beach landing sites runs over pretty flat terrain to the Tadji airstrips, less than a mile away. Air reconnaissance indicates the road is solid enough to accommodate heavy vehicles, so we ought to take those airstrips in a hurry. We'll have at least one tank battalion and one artillery battalion for support."

14

Krueger scanned the officers around him before he continued. "The One fourteenth Combat Engineer Battalion will make the initial landing with the One sixty-third RCT to work on those Tadji airstrips as soon as combat infantry troops have occupied the fields. Let's hope we have the strips secured by dark."

"We don't expect too much trouble at Aitape," General MacArthur said. "G-two says the enemy only has a couple thousand troops there and most of these are service troops working on the airfields. We doubt if more than a batallion of them are combat troops, so the enemy is not likely to offer much opposition."

"Charlie," Krueger looked at General Hall, "as soon as you secure the Tadji airstrips, I want you to send out at least one reinforced combat battalion to the Nigia River, five miles to the east, and set up a defense perimeter. The Japanese may attempt to send reinforcements up the coast."

"Okay," Hall nodded.

"As I said, we'll have an RCT from the Thirty-second and the One twelfth Cavalry RCT in reserve. In fact, we may land some of these troops on L plus one if it becomes necessary. In any event these units will relieve the One sixty-third by L plus fourteen."

"That'll be fine," General Hall said.

General MacArthur now turned to the Fifth Air Force commander. "George, we'll need a thorough job from your airmen if these operations are to succeed. You'll need to neutralize the airfields at Wewak, Hollandia, and at Wakde-Sarme.''

"That's a big order," Kenney said.

"It has to be done," MacArthur said. "We'll have those navy planes for the invasion itself, but we want those enemy airfields neutralized before we make the landings on April 22. We must continue sustained, multiple air strikes over a two or three week period."

"Right now we've got about eight hundred fighters and eight hundred bombers in the Fifth Air Force Command," Kenney said, "but only about 70 percent of these planes are operable at any given time. We've been hitting the Japanese airfields at Hansa Bay and Alexishafen pretty hard and we've pretty much put them out of commission. The Nips don't even keep planes there anymore. We've also been working over the Wewak bases at But and Boram quite regularly and we hope to have these bases out of commission by the time of the invasions. But, I can't promise the same thing for the Hollandia and Wakde-Sarmi fields."

"It's got to be done," MacArthur insisted.

"We'll do our best," Kenney answered.

"All right, gentlemen," the SWPA CinC said, "get back to your commanders and get them thoroughly acquainted with these operations. I'll expect air and naval units to start softening the target areas by April 1. I also want Wewak especially hard hit so the Japanese will think we'll be making our landing attempts there."

"From our intelligence reports, the Japanese

apparently expect our next move to be against the Wewak area," General Krueger said. "The enemy has been withdrawing troops from forward bases at Madang and Alexishafen and moving them westward across the Ramu and Sepik Rivers to Wewak and Hansa Bay. So, we'd like them to go on thinking we'll invade Wewak." He looked at Kenney. "As General MacArthur suggested, Fifth Air Force should intensify its assaults on Wewak. Anyway, if you hit Wewak badly enough, you'll prevent the Japanese from using the Wewak airfield when we make the twin landings on April 22 far up the coast."

Krueger then turned to Admiral Barbey. "It would also be a good idea to bombard the Hansa Bay area with surface ships, and you might increase PT boat patrols along the Madang-Wewak coastline."

"We even intend to drop dummy parachutes into the vicinity," MacArthur said, "and to leave empty rubber rafts in the Wewak area to make the Japanese think that reconnaissance patrols are active in the area. In fact, the amphibious task forces will sail toward Wewak, but during the night the vessels will turn north and swing southwest. The ships will then split, with both amphibious groups arriving at their target areas on the early morning of April 22. This maneuver will require a two-hundred-mile detour and an extra day at sea. But," the SWPA commander gestured, "this added movement will convince the Japanese that we're heading

17

for Wewak. We should catch the enemy garrisons at Hollandia and Aitape pretty much off guard."

"Any questions?" General Krueger asked.

None.

"Good," the 6th Army commander nodded. "We'll start immediately to move the Twenty-fourth and Sixth Divisions along with the Five hundred second RCT to Goodenough Island. The Forty-first Division will move to Cape Cretin here in the Admiralties, and the Thirty-second units and the One twelfth Cavalry will stage out of Saidor below Madang. Meanwhile, the Australian troops will continue to put pressure on the Japanese at Madang. That should keep the enemy's Eighteenth Army neutralized in the Wewak-Madang area during the landings at Hollandia and Aitape."

Some of the officers at the table nodded, but none of them answered Gen. Walter Krueger.

The conference at Cape Cretin continued through the next few days as the generals met with subordinates, down to regiment and battalion commanders, to work out details of their particular jobs in the operations. They studied maps, requisitioned supplies, rations and arms, and familiarized themselves with landing areas. They also checked transport accommodations to make certain they had enough room for troops and supplies. And finally, staff officers carefully studied aerial photographs and reconnaissance reports to make certain they were thoroughly acquainted with the landing sites in their particular areas.

Then rehearsals began for the twin invasions. The 24th, 6th, and 502nd practiced their amphibious landing techniques at Tangota Bay on the south side of Goodenough Island, while the 41st Division's RCT which would land at Humboldt Bay at Hollandia rehearsed at Cape Cretin on the Admiralties.

The 163rd RCT and the RCTs of the 32nd Division and 116th Cavalry, who were assigned to Aitape, practiced amphibious operations on the long, sandy shorelines between Saidor and Finchhaven in Papuan New Guinea since the terrain was similar to the long, flat shoreline of the Aitape area. The 3rd Battalion of the 163rd also set up simulated defenses along the Kalapit River southeast of Saidor, the kind of defense they would need to maintain on the Nigia River at Aitape against any Japanese attempt to retake the area.

Gen. George Kenney, meanwhile, worked with his 5th Air Force group commanders to get his air units into operations against Hollandia and Aitape. Kenney first alerted his heavy bomb groups to stage out of Natzab near Moresby for long, 600-mile flights to bomb the Wakde-Sarmi airfields every day, weather permitting. The 5th Air Force commander hoped the B-24s would so saturate these bases north of Hollandia that the Japanese could not mount air intervention against the American invaders at Tanahmerah and Humboldt Bays.

Kenney also moved the bulk of his 5th Air Force medium and light bomber groups to Nadzab above Lae to put them within range of Hollandia. The air commander also ordered modifications on the P-38 fighter planes of his 49th and 475th Fighter Groups to increase range. Aviation engineers of the 5th Air Service Command at their depot in Townsville, Australia, worked during the last two weeks of March to complete the technical changes. The P-38 Lightnings could then fly over 900 miles and thus escort bombers to Hollandia, some 425 miles from Nadzab.

On April 1, Kenney again called together this group commanders at the 5th Air Force AD-VON headquarters in Port Moresby, New Guinea.

"I want the heavies to concentrate on the Wakde-Sarmi airfields," Kenney said, "because the enemy seems to be working overtime to complete several runways in that area. Our recon reports suggest similar activities at Hollandia."

Kenney looked at some sheets of paper on his desk before he continued. "Our latest counts shows that we have 177 B-twenty-fours among our Forty-third, Ninetieth, Twenty-second, and Three-eightieth Heavy Bomb Groups. The Three-eightieth at Darwin will begin hitting Wakde-Sarmi tomorrow and the other twelve heavy bomb squadrons here in New Guinea will start hitting Wakde-Sarmi as soon as we have favorable weather. We've also got one-hundred-thirty operable B-twenty-fives between the Thirty-eighth and Three-hundred-forty-fifth Groups and one hundred seven-five combat ready A-twentys among the third Group at Nadzab, the four-hundred seventeenth at Dobodura, and the Three twelfth Group at Gufsap. The Four-Seventh will move its A-twentys to Saidor at once, and that will put our entire complement of B-twenty-fives and A-twentys within range of Hollandia.''

"What about our fighters?" Lt. Col. Charles MacDonald of the 475th Fighter Group asked.

"Since all three fighter groups have been altered for long range flights," Kenney said, "they'll be used mostly as escort. Your own 475 Group and the P-thirty-eights of the Forty-ninth Fighter Group will be responsible for escorting light and medium bombers on the Hollandia missions. The Thirty-fifth Fighter Group will be responsible for escorting bombers for strikes on the Wewak airdromes and for strikes in the Aitape area.''

"Yes, sir," Lt. Colonel MacDonald said.

"In fact," Kenney continued, "if time permits, we may have the P-thirty-eights of the Thirty-fifth Group also converted for long range escort duty. I've already ordered Lt. Col. Ed Gavin of the Four eighty-second Service Squadron to come to Nadzab with a team of men so they can work on the Thirty-fifth's Lightnings." He looked at another sheet on his desk. "The Eighth, Four seventy-fifth Groups have One forty-sixth operational long range P-Thirty-eighths. If Lt. Colonel Gavin and his men work quickly, they might have another fifty P-Thirty-eights available for long range escort duty to Hollandia during the preinvasion aerial assaults.''

Kenney scanned his group commanders before he spoke again. "I want to emphasize one point," he gestured, "while the runways at Wewak and in the Wakde-Sarmi areas are fair game, try to avoid destroying the runways and taxiways at Aitape and Hollandia. We'll want to use these airstrips as soon as possible after our ground troops secure them. Concentrate your attacks on grounded aircraft, anti-aircraft positions, and artillery positions. You should also pinpoint shoreline and inland defense positions, troop concentrations, and supply depots. We intend to use one A-twenty group exclusively for hitting the Japanese barge traffic up and down the New Guinea coast. We may also use one of the P-Thirty-eight groups for this purpose.''

"We understand," Lt. Col. Richard Ellis of the 3rd Bomb Group said.

"Good," Kenney nodded. "Any questions?"

"All we need are the flight orders, sir," Lt. Colonel MacDonald said.

"We'll start cutting FOs tomorrow and by the day after we'll get this aerial show on the road. If we do our jobs, the Japanese won't even be able to respond to Operations Reckless and Persecution with anything more than mere rifle fire.''

"Let's hope so, sir," Lt. Colonel Ellis said.

While Kenney worked with his 5th Air Force commanders, both Gen. Robert Eichelberger and Gen. Charles Hall worked with their respective 1st Corps and IX Corps troops. The two corps commanders watched the rehearsals of their combat teams with satisfaction. Further, both commanders were satisfied with logistics—enough troops, supplies, arms, and transports for the Hollandia and Aitape operations. They expected little trouble with Japanese resistance. With such ample resources and good training, why should they have too many problems?

However, the Japanese would not accept the American invasions passively. When the Nippon brass recovered from the shock of these daring American amphibious operations, their response would stun both Eichelberger and Hall, along with Gen. Douglas MacArthur himself.

Chapter Two

Gen. Hatazo Adachi, commander of the Japanese 18th Army in New Guinea, had probably suffered more frustrations than any general in the Imperial Armed Forces. For nearly a year and a half, Adachi had experienced one misfortune after another, and Imperial General Headquarters had all but abandoned him.

Early in the war, Adachi had led victorious Japanese forces in massive sweeps through the East Indies, New Britain, and New Guinea, causing more anxiety for the Allies than any other Japanese commander. Even while the Japanese Imperial Navy had been suffering defeats in the Battles of the Coral Sea and Midway, and even while other army commanders had crumbled before the Americans in the Solomons, Adachi had continued to move forward.

The 18th Army commander had capped his series of brilliant successes with the capture of Buna in July of 1942 and then the astounding march over the Owen Stanley Mountains of New Guinea. By September of 1942, Adachi's victorious army had come within 30 miles of Port Moresby, the last Allied outpost north of Australia. The Japanese high command had grudgingly admitted that Adachi had triumphed where other navy and army commanders had failed.

Hatazo Adachi had always been an outsider among the Japanese military commanders. He had come from common stock rather than from the Imperial military stock that had dominated the leadership of the Japanese armed forces for centuries. He had never won a Samurai award and his crude, country mien seemed out of place among the more refined, sophisticated aristocrats who had risen to high positions in the Imperial army and navy. Adachi had been born and raised among the lower caste people in the small farming village of Yoshino on the island of Shikoku. Tradition should have condemned him to a simple agrarian life. However, he had been blessed with high intelligence and good academic ability. Thus, when he finished school in Yoshino, an officer friend of the family had wheedled an appointment for him to the Central Military Academy in Tokyo.

During his first year at the school, fellow students from more prestigious and wealthy backgrounds had ignored the coarse Adachi. However, the farm boy from Yoshino, through sheer determination and ability, had not only excelled in academics, but also in sports and military activities. He had then risen so rapidly in the army that by 1941 he had won command of the elite Imperial 51st Infantry Division, a unit still under his command in April of 1944.

Adachi's division had succeeded so thoroughly during the opening months of the war that by the spring of 1942, Gen. Hitoshi Imamura, commander of the 8th Area Forces, had given him command of the new 18th Japanese Army. The grateful Adachi had not disappointed Imamura, for the 18th Army had overrun most of the Bismarck Archipelago and had completed the impossible task of crossing New Guinea's treacherous Owen Stanleys to threaten Australia.

The continuous success of the 18th Army had prompted his troops to call Adachi ''The Unconquerable,'' and his men worshipped Adachi second only to the Emperor himself. This same success, however, had generated more envy than admiration from other Imperial commanders, many of whom secretly hoped that Adachi would fail somewhere along the line.

These jealous officers got their wish when Adachi suffered the disastrous defeat at Buna after the sixth month Papuan campaign. In fact, from 1943 on, Adachi had endured only further reversals: the loss of a reinforcement convoy in the Battle of the Bismarck Sea, the loss of Lae, Cape Gloucester, Arawe, and Finchhaven. The 18th Army fell into steady retreat up the New Guinea coast.

Adachi had begged for help to stem the worsening situation in New Guinea, but his pleas had fallen on deaf ears. The Japanese simply did not have the means to aid him. Reinforcements in men, supplies, arms, and aircraft had come to Adachi in dribbles, hardly enough to maintain his army, much less stop the persistent Allied offensives.

Then, with the Allies' successful reduction of Rabaul, General Imamura, Adachi's only real friend in the Pacific, had himself fallen into disfavor with Imperial General Headquarters. The 18th Army commander was left in the Wewak area of New Guinea with some 50,000 troops to cope as best he could against the rapidly increasing Allied strength.

In March of 1944, Adachi was ordered to Manado in the Celebes Islands, the headquarters of the 2nd Area Forces. Also ordered to Manado was Adachi's 6th Air Division commander, Gen. Giichi Itabana, whose headquarters was also at Wewak. The 18th Army commander was surprised by the summons since his army was under the jurisdiction of the 8th Area Forces in the now defused stronghold of Rabaul.

Gen. Korechika Anami commanded the 2nd Area Forces and he had recently moved his headquarters from Davao in the Philippines to Manado in the Celebes. As soon as Adachi arrived in Manado, Anami held a private meeting with the 18th Army commander. "General, perhaps you are surprised to be called here, but IGH has made some changes in command structure. We have received a directive from Imperial Headquarters in Tokyo, and I have called a conference here to discuss a strategy that deals with all units of the Second Area Forces."

"But what has that to do with me?" Adachi asked. "My Eighteenth Army and my Sixth Air Division are under jurisdiction of the Eighth Area Forces."

Anami pursed his lips soberly. "Your army is now under the jurisdiction of the Second Area Forces." When Adachi frowned, Anami handed the 18th Army commander a sheet of paper, an order from IGH in Japan. "IGH has devised a new strategy for the southern area and the Eighteenth Army has been included in this plan."

Adachi read the directive and then squeezed his face. "But we have been under the Eighth Area command for more than two years. Why has IGH made this sudden transfer?"

"The new plan calls for the establishment of a revised defense perimeter in the southern sector to contain further enemy encroachments into our inner empire. Your army, general, will play a role in this strategy."

"I have a disheartening suspicion that IGH has abandoned the Honorable Imamura, along with eastern New Guinea, New Britain, and the Solomons."

General Anami only pursed his lips again; he did not answer.

"I would rather remain under Imamura's command. Together we enjoyed victories and suffered defeats. Together we have known elation and despair. If the Eighth Area Forces are to be deserted, I prefer to wither away with them."

"It cannot be," Anami said. "Your fo[...] too important and too experienced for su[...] fate." The 2nd Area Forces commander lean[...] closer to Adachi and stared at him with a tinge of sympathy. "I realize the great loyalty you held for General Imamura, and I know that you enjoyed a mutual trust and respect with the honorable commander. But," Anami gestured, "we must be realistic. We can no longer talk of new invasions and new offensives. We have suffered severe losses in men, aircraft, ships, and supplies over the past year. No one can be more aware of this than you. Our entire strategy now calls for defensive measures to hold fast our remaining territories. We must stop the Americans from cutting or even invading the East Indies from which we obtain most of our oil, tin, and other raw materials. Surely, you understand this."

"Yes," Adachi answered.

"No one has more admiration and respect for Imamura than have I," Anami gestured, "but the truth is evident. We have lost the Bismarck Archipelago, we have lost the Solomons, and Rabaul has been reduced to impotency. Because of our enemy's great strength, we are in no position to reverse these losses. You must abide by the decisions of IGH, whose authority comes from the Emperor himself."

"Of course," Adachi said with resignation.

"Good," General Anami smiled. "We will begin our conference tomorrow to discuss this new stategy."

29

On the morning of March 20 1944, after a good breakfast, Gen. Korechika Anami opened the conference at his 2nd Area Forces headquarters in Manado. Adachi found an array of other military commanders here: Gen. Fusatoro Teshima, who commanded the 2nd Army in the East Indies; Gen. Kunichi Teramoto, commander of the 4th Air Army; Gen. Masazumi Inada of the 2nd Field Base in Hollandia; and Adm. Yoshikazu Endo, commander of the 9th Fleet. When the various commanders had settled themselves, Anami began.

"We have received new instructions from IGH in Tokyo. I have spent some days with them and they have agreed to a new strategy for the southern area. We will initiate Operational Order A-forty-six, a defensive plan to stop further enemy incursions against our inner empire, especially the East Indies and the Philippines. The loss of the Indies or the Philippines could bring ruination to our war effort, so every last son of Japan must pledge a new resolve to protect these territories."

The commanders sat mute, only listening, while Anami continued. "My aides will pass out copies of OO A-forty-six and you can read the plan for yourselves while we discuss the strategy. IGH has marked off a new defensive line and we are ordered to hold this perimeter at all costs." He gestured to the officers before he continued. "You can see from the map on the face page that the boundary between the Eight Area and Second Area Forces jurisdiction has been moved eastward to one forty-seven degrees longitude. This revised boundary in effect places the Eighteenth Army and its Sixth Air Division under the control of the Second Area Forces."

The A-46 plan had apparently conceded the loss of New Britain, the Solomons, Kavieng, Rabaul, and eastern New Guinea. The plan also hinted strongly that the 17th Army in the Solomons and the other 8th Area Forces in New Britain and Rabaul were irretrievably cut off. The IGH directive simply stated that forces in these areas would simply sustain themselves as best they could until or if they could be reinforced or evacuated.

The A-46 plan outlined a retracted defensive perimeter. The strategic line of resistance would now extend from the Japanese home islands down through the Bonin Islands group, the Marianna chain, Ponape, Truk, the Paulaus chain, into the Celebes, and then through New Guinea as far as Wewak. The 2nd Area Forces would hold all territories east and north of this line. The directive further called for protective air and sea bases on the Vogelkop Peninsula at the westernmost tip of New Guinea, on the Lesser Soenda Islands, the Aebe Islands in the Arafura Sea, Wakde-Sarmi, Hollandia, and Wewak to the south. The plan also called for the withdrawal of forces from Madang, south of Wewak, while the Japanese built Hollandia into a major supply and air base.

Imperial General Headquarters had also asked that strong air bases be developed at Wakde-

Sarmi and Hollandia, a task that General Anami had already begun, and an operation already verified by the U.S. 5th Air Force reconnaissance.

"Imperial Headquarters is sending us the Thirty-second and Thirty-fifth Infantry Divisions," General Anami continued. "The Thirty-second will build defense positions in the Halmaheras and the Thirty-fifth Division will move to western New Guinea. Halmahera must be impregnable because the island will be the principal distribution point to supply the East Indies and western New Guinea with men, arms, aircraft, and supplies."

Operational Order A-46 also called for strong air defenses, a responsibility of the 4th Air Army that had also moved its headquarters from Davao to the Celebes. The 4th would be at Amboina, about 50 miles south of the 2nd Area Forces headquarters at Manado. Gen. Kunachi Teramoto, who had served in Manchuria, Southeast Asia, and the Philippines, was an experienced army air officer. He had always managed to get the most out of his air units against the increasing Allied air superiority. The 6th Air Division would not be assigned to Teramoto and General Itabana, like his 18th Army commander, had resigned himself to this new command.

The 4th Air Army had assumed responsibility for developing the airfields at Wakde-Sarmi, Hollandia, and Aitape. The 4th would also supply air protection for western New Guinea and for the eastern islands of the Dutch East Indies.

By March of 1944, the 4th Air Army had about 750 planes under its command, including the aircraft of the newly absorbed 6th Air Division. However, this number was less than half the number of the opposing U.S. 5th Air Force. Further, many of these Japanese planes were inoperable because they lacked parts or adequate service facilities. Nonetheless, General Teramoto had set up a plan to resist any new Allied attacks within the newly established OO A-46 perimeter.

The 4th Air Army commander had decided to keep the 6th Air Division in New Guinea with its more than 400 planes, concentrating these aircraft at Wakde-Sarmi, Hollandia, and Aitape. The 4th's 7th Air Division with about 300 planes would remain in reserve at the Galela Drome in the Halmaheras and at Kamiri Drome on Noemfoor Island.

Teramoto would instruct General Itabana to station his three air units of the 6th Division as follows: the 8th Air Brigade on the Vogelkop Peninsula at the western extreme of New Guinea, the 14th Air Brigade at Wakde-Sarmi, and the 30th Air Brigade at Hollandia. IGH in Tokyo had assured General Teramoto of more aircraft. As soon as the 4th Air Army commander received these plans he would distribute them between the 6th and 7th Air Divisions. If Teramoto got the 500 new aircraft he requested, he believed he could stop any further Allied invasion threats in the Southwest Pacific area.

Admiral Endo's 9th Fleet would be responsible for patrolling the New Guinea coastline from the tip of the Vokelkop Peninsula down to Wewak. Endo's job was to report and even stop any Allied naval forces that moved up the New Guinea coast. However, since the Imperial navy expected heavy sea engagements in the Central and Western Pacific they had sent no reinforcements to the 9th Fleet. Endo's flotillas included little more than a motley array of sub chasers, a half dozen mine sweepers, a few submarines, and about a hundred barges. This meager force was unlikely to stop even the smallest American flotilla that always included heavy warships. In fact, Adm. Daniel Barbey's own U.S. TF 77 which patrolled the New Guinea coast line included four Australian heavy cruisers and a dozen American destroyers. This Allied fleet could easily dispose of anything in the Japanese 9th Fleet.

As General Anami outlined the A-46 plan, General Adachi noted the obvious omissions to Wewak: no reinforcements in men, supplies, or planes, and no 9th Fleet patrols south of Wewak. Adachi was especially piqued because the plan did not call for build-ups at the Wewak air bases as well as the build-ups at Hollandia and Wakde-Sarmi. He questioned the 2nd Area Forces commander.

"Honorable Anami, this order requests that the Sixth Air Division will only maintain its air brigades at Vogelkop, Wakde-Sarmi, and Hollandia, and no mention is made of Captain

Akamatsu's Two forty-eighth Flying Regiment at Wewak. Nor is there any mention of sending more supplies to Wewak. We have fifty thousand troops at Wewak and these men need more provisions and more air cover. How can we expect to maintain a strong position there without such reinforcements?''

General Anami pursed his lips before he spoke. "I suggest, general, that you look at the next page of the order. I must tell you that IGH has suggested a possible withdrawal of troops from Wewak and not a reinforcement. We know the Two forty-eighth Flying Regiment is badly depleted, and I frankly believe that this unit should be withdrawn to Hollandia to join the Thirtieth Air Brigade. We would also request, general, that you retire all troops from the Madang and Hansa Bay areas and bring them across the Sepik River to concentrate them north of Wewak. Finally, I had planned to ask that you send two of your divisions overland from Wewak to Hollandia to join elements of the Thirty-fifth Division in strengthening defenses there.''

"What?" Adachi gasped. "This plan does say we will hold a line from Wewak north and yet you want to abandon Wewak as we did the rest of the Bismark Archipelago?''

"No," Anami said. "We do ask that you prepare defenses in the Wewak area with your remaining division of the Eighteenth Army.''

"One division? And no aircraft?" Adachi barked angrily. "Are you planning to abandon me as IGH abandoned General Imamura?"

"You could move your headquarters to Hollandia."

"General Anami," Adachi protested, "the enemy has been building its forces and conducting amphibious exercises at Saidor, according to our scouting reports. They also have troops in the Admiralties who are conducting similar amphibious exercises. This means that the enemy plans a new invasion soon. This attempt can only come in the Wewak area. It is of the utmost importance that we have enough troops, arms, supplies, and aircraft to repel such an invasion."

Anami did not immediately answer; nor did the others about the conference table . . . not General Teshina of the 2nd Army, Admiral Endo of the 9th Fleet, General Inada of the 2nd Field Base, or General Teramoto of the 4th Air Army. Even Brig. General Itabana of Adachi's own 6th Air Division said nothing. The officers simply sat soberly, apparently unwilling to get involved in the obvious confrontation between Anami and Adachi.

The 18th Army commander half scowled at the silent faces and then turned again to the 2nd Area Forces commander. "I implore you, Honorable Anami, do not abandon Wewak. It is the final defensive outpost against our enemies. My troops are experienced, they are determined, and they will fight to the end. Half of the fifty thousand men in the Wewak area are trained jungle fighters. If we strengthen the Wewak

36

area, I am certain the enemy cannot dislodge us as they have conquered other areas in the Solomons and Bismarck Archipelago. I would remind you again," he gestured, "that the A-forty-six order does specify that Wewak will be the most forward outpost of this new defense perimeter."

Adachi now scanned the sober men about the conference table. "None of you here can dispute my suspicion that the enemy will attempt to invade Wewak. Yet, I have heard no support from any of you. I can only conclude that you are willing to leave a division of the Eighteenth Army there to become sacrificial lambs so that you can strengthen your positions northwest of Wewak."

When the men at the table still did not answer the 18th Army commander, Adachi's neck reddened in anger and he glowered at the officers. "What do any of you truly know about the agony and death and disappointment of men in combat who must fight day after day against a strong and aggressive enemy? Who among you has been forced to fight ten times your number in enemy troops, guns, ships, and aircraft, while he ate grubs and wild grasses because he had no supplies? How many of you have suffered almost daily surface ship bombardments and enemy air strikes for week after week and month after month?"

The conferees did not answer, but now their faces softened in sympathy.

"No," Adachi gestured dramatically, "you

37

have never experienced this agony. You sit back in the safety of these rear areas and enjoy your leisures and comforts with plenty of food, recreation facilities, and geisha girls to entertain you. Do not tell me how to defend New Guinea with your theories that fit so neatly into place in academy classrooms, or with your artfully drawn maps that look so impressive. My troops have fought the enemy for two years. We understand them and we know them. You want two of these experienced divisions while you abandon the third. But I tell you," Adachi now banged a fist on the table, "I will not abandon a single one of these soldiers in Wewak without doing all I can to strengthen them as fully as possible to meet new enemy threats."

Adachi then straightened fully and hardened his face. "If you abandon these men, you must abandon me, for I will not leave them so long as a single Eighteenth Army soldier still breathes at Wewak."

The sober men now lowered their faces, obviously embarrassed by their silence.

"Do not abandon us at Wewak," Adachi continued, speaking softly now. "If you do, I can assure you that the enemy will next strike Aitape, then Hollandia, then Wadka-Sarmi, and even this pleasant Celebes Island on which you live in comfortable luxury."

General Itabana now looked up at the 18th Army commander. "Honorable Adachi, I have shamed myself for not speaking in your defense. But let me say now that I too will remain in

Wewak until the last airman of the Two forty-eighth Flying Regiment breathes his last. You are correct in not wanting to abandon Wewak."

Itabana's support prompted General Teshino of the 2nd Army to speak. "Please accept my apologies, Honorable Adachi. I was gravely at fault for not considering the plight of your brave fighting men and the need to do all we can for them."

General Anami could see the growing compassion for Adachi and he felt uneasy. He knew well the reputation of Adachi, the loyalty of his troops, and the respect that people in Japan felt for him. He was sure that others here would soon follow General Teshino in support of Adachi. Further, Anami recognized the importance of Adachi's cooperation for strategy A-46. If he did not get the 18th Army commander to work fully with him, the 2nd Area commander would need to relieve Adachi of command. Repercussions for such action would reach Japan, and Japanese civilians as well as many in the military would become incensed by the degradation of the popular 18th Army commander.

Actually, General Anami had leeway in the A-46 plan, including the authority to make changes wherever he saw fit. He now realized he would need to alter the plan to satisfy the 18th Army commander.

"I am willing to listen to you, Honorable Adachi," Anami said. "Perhaps you might suggest some changes for this plan."

"I appreciate such an opportunity," Adachi said. "I am willing to move one division up the coast to Hollandia, but I must keep at least two divisions in Wewak. I will abandon Madang, but we must have supplies to strengthen our defenses in Wewak. Finally, while I agree to the Sixth Air Division move to Hollandia, I must insist that we keep the Two forty-eighth Flying Regiment at Wewak and that we get replacements in aircraft for this air regiment."

"Perhaps this can be done," Anami nodded.

"We want at least fifty new fighters and bombers."

"We will give you these if possible," General Teramoto said.

"I am also concerned that the Ninth Fleet intends to maintain its patrols only as far as Wewak and not down to Madang and even Saidor."

"It was our feeling, Honorable Adachi," Admiral Endo said, "that it would be too dangerous to send our small vessels as far south as Saidor because of the heavy enemy air and sea patrols in the Huon Gulf area."

"Admiral," Adachi scowled, "we cannot prepare ourselves for an enemy invasion if we do not maintain patrols south of Wewak. I would remind you, the airmen and soldiers of the Eighteenth Army have suffered miserably from air attacks, jungle warfare, and a lack of food and medicine. They do not complain. They do not refuse to make jungle patrols or to fly aerial reconnaissance because the Allies have superior numbers in men and planes. Are the sailors of the Ninth Fleet so timid that they cannot face such superior enemy forces?''

Admiral Endo lowered his head. ''I feel ashamed, general. You are correct. The Ninth Fleet must not waver from its duty. We will patrol along the New Guinea coast as far south as necessary.''

General Adachi nodded and then sat down.

Now, General Anami again addressed the officers. ''It was obvious that General Adachi's suggestions must be heeded, for he has fought the enemy for many months and he understands them. We will ask the Forth Air Army to make every effort to send reinforcements in men and planes to the Two forty-eighth Flying Regiment. Admiral Endo's vessels will patrol as far as Saidor.'' Anami then looked at General Teshino. ''You will move the Thirty-sixth Division to Hollandia and the Wadka-Sarmi area as soon as feasible, while we strengthen all of our air bases as much as possible, from the Vogelkop Peninsula to Wewak.''

''Yes, Honorable Anami,'' General Teshino said.

''Meanwhile elements of the Fifty-first Division will move to Hollandia, while the Twentieth and Forty-first Divisions of the Eighteenth Army will remain in Wewak. Will such changes in the A-forty-six plan be satisfactory.'' Anami asked Adachi.

''Yes,'' the 18th Army Commander nodded.

Anami, then turned to the others. ''Is there

41

anything further that any of you wish to discuss?'' None answered and Anami looked at Adachi. ''General?''

''No,'' Adachi said, ''except that I would also ask that you send new supplies to Wewak as soon as possible, and as many provisions as you can.''

''We will do all we can,'' Anami promised. Then he sighed. ''If there is no further discussion, this conference is over. We will retire for tea and rice cakes.''

The commander of the 2nd Area Forces had been wise to heed Adachi's pleas, even if Anami disapproved personally. Within three weeks, Anami would get the shock of his life. The very survival of the 2nd Area Forces would depend on Adachi's battle tested troops of the 18th Army.

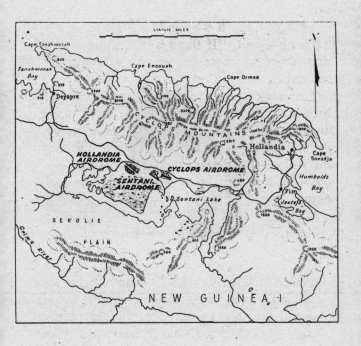

Hollandia in April of 1944, where Japanese had big base, including three airdromes

Chapter Three

The terrain of the U.S. invasion targets were similar in many ways. Hollandia and Aitape, both on the north coast of New Guinea, received heavy rainfall, about 100 inches a year. Both area consisted of mostly jungle, with hot humid climates, and every conceivable type of tropical insect to harass a human being. Inhabitants included mostly natives, and the few whites who had fled the area before the Japanese juggernaut early in the war. Finally, the Toricelli Mountains of the Owen Stanley range rose into dense, forested, hostile peaks to the south of both areas.

Hollandia, however, offered a diversified landscape as opposed to the flat, coastal terrain at Aitape. Hollandia included two excellent bays, a beautiful highland lake, and a flat oblong of terrain behind the lake. A ring of mountains arced around the entire Hollandia complex on the west, south, and east laterals, leaving only the seacoast open for heavy traffic.

The two sheltered harbors, Humboldt Bay and Tanahmerah Bay, about 25 miles apart, were separated by the Cyclops Mountains whose coastal peaks rose to 7,000 feet before dropping to an almost sheer cliff into the Pacific Ocean. Both Humboldt and Tanahmerah could anchor at least a hundred large ships each. Thus, if the Americans took the region, they could supply and defend Hollandia with huge armadas. Further, the shorelines of these two bays possessed sandy beaches for easy amphibious landings or for barge traffic.

On the south side of the Cyclops Mountains, beyond the bay and through some fifteen miles of uphill jungles, lay the crescent shaped Lake Sentani, some 15 miles long and five to six miles wide. Along the lake's south shoreline was the Sentani Plateau, a huge, flat area that ended at the foothills of the Toricelli Mountains. The plains, despite heavy rainfall, were relatively dry and exceptionally suited for the construction and maintenance of airfields.

Invaders could only come by sea and they

would need to approach Hollandia through the two bays that could be easily defended. Inland, the rugged slopes of the Toricelli Mountains ruled out invasion by any overland route. Only a few jungle trails ran into Hollandia from the east and west. A strong defensive position on the Tami River to the east or on the Grime River on the west could easily thwart any movement into the Lake Sentani Plateau over these trails.

No wonder, then, after their reverses in the Bismarck Archipelago during the past year, the Japanese had selected this region as a good area in which to build new supply, harbor, and air installations.

The Japanese had first occupied Hollandia in April of 1942, two years ago, but they had ignored the region for many months. However, as their fortunes worsened in Eastern New Guinea, the Solomons, and New Britain, the Japanese had taken a closer look at Hollandia. By 1944, the Japanese had completed three airfields on the Sentani Plateau and they had begun construction of a fourth at Tami, at the eastern edge of the plains.

Further, as shipping lanes became untenable in the Bismarck Sea because of Allied naval superiority, the Japanese had developed Humboldt Bay into a major anchorage and supply point. Large ships unloaded here and then barges carried arms and supplies along the coast, mostly at night, to feed the Japanese garrisons to the east as far down as Wewak, 205 miles away.

In contrast to Hollandia, Aitape was a flat rectangle, with a 2,000 yard wide length of beach. The level terrain, about five miles wide and a dozen miles long, ran from the X-ray-Koronal River on the east to the Raiho River on the west. Beyond the oblong plain, on both east and west, lay nothing but remote, dense, swampy, steaming jungles with nothing more than native trails that were often inundated after heavy rainfalls. Along the southern rim of Aitape, the hostile jungle slopes of the Toricelli Mountains totally sheltered the area.

Before World War II, Aitape had been a small native village with a few wooden structures to house local Australian officials. Aside from inter-island trading in bird-of-paradise feathers, Aitape had no business enterprise. During the 1930s, the Australian government had endeavored to promote colonization and agriculture at Aitape, but the balky stone age natives had refused to till the soil, preferring their nomadic, wild jungle lives. White settlers themselves rarely stayed here long because of Aitape's distasteful climate and remote location. By 1936, except for the Tadji Coconut Plantation, Aitape had diminished to insignificance. Only a few brave explorers occasionally came here to conduct prospecting or map making expeditions in the New Guinea interior.

The Japanese had not occupied Aitape until December of 1942 when they sent a small complement of engineers and a company of combat troops here to set up camp outside the native village of Wapili at the northeast corner of the coconut plantation. Imperial Japanese Headquarters had attached little importance to the region except for a possible airfield on the plantation flats, if any such airstrip became necessary.

With the loss of Japanese bases to the east and in the Bismarck Archipelago, Aitape had gained new importance. As the Japanese strengthened their defenses at Wewak and Madang to the east, and as they built up Hollandia in Dutch New Guinea, the 2nd Area Forces Headquarters in Davao decided to build two airstrips at Aitape, a fighter strip and a bomber strip. Fighter planes at Aitape could then escort bombers coming down from Hollandia to attack Allied bases in eastern New Guinea. Further, the runways at Tadji could serve as staging areas for aircraft flying between Wewak and Hollandia.

Eighty miles of jungle lay between Aitape and Wewak, with only coastal trails to link the two areas. Further, a series of rivers, the Driniumor, Koronal, and X-ray, cut through the jungles east of Tadji. A military force at Aitape could set up excellent defense positions on the banks of these rivers and presumably stop any hostile troops moving westward through the jungle from Wewak. So, if the Americans occupied Aitape, they were certain they could set up perimeters on these rivers and stop any serious threat from the Japanese at Wewak.

The Japanese, of course, believed with near certainty that the next Allied thrust would come against Wewak. So while the 2nd Area Forces worked intently to build up Hollandia and Aitape, they had failed to provide any real protection to these areas with enough combat troops. By April of 1944, the Japanese had completed their build-up at Hollandia and the 4th Air Army had moved dozens of aircrafts into the Lake Sentani airdromes. Vessels were now sailing regularly in and out of Humboldt Bay to unload arms, food, and supplies for distribution to Japanese units on the New Guinea coast. However, of the 11,000 men at Hollandia by April 1 only a mere reinforced battalion, about 1,000 troops, were combat forces. Further, the 2nd Area Forces had sent less than a battery of artillery and anti-aircraft guns to Hollandia.

Only the Matsuyuma Force from the 36th Division's 224th infantry Regiment had arrived in Hollandia. Other units of this combat division were not expected to arrive until about April 30. Most of the division was still in the East Indies with only another battalion of the 224th Regiment as far east as Wakde-Sarmi. At Aitape, protective measures were practically nil. Less than a thousand soldiers occupied the area with only about 200 of them combat troops. They only possessed a mere dozen light artillery pieces.

The real preparations for combat were to the southwest at Wewak. By April 1, Gen. Hatazo Adachi had begun to evacuate Madang and Hansa Bay, south of Wewak, while he strengthened Wewak itself, especially around the two airdromes at Boram and But. Further, because of the expected threat to Wewak, Adachi had procrastinated on moving a full division north to Hollandia. He had thus far only sent one battalion northward. The 3rd Battalion of the 20th Division, under Lt. Col. Masanasobu Tsuji, had only reached Yakamul, some 25 miles from Aitape, and Adachi was in no hurry to move them any faster. Tsuji, an experienced jungle fighter in the Malayan campaign, merely encamped at Yakamul to await further orders from the 18th Army commander.

Anami had not been overly concerned about the delay in moving the Division from Wewak to Hollandia. He, like everyone else in the 2nd Area Forces, was certain the Americans would attempt to invade Wewak. In fact, Anami had not even complained because the 36th Division had moved quite slowly into Hollandia. He was more interested in the 4th Air Army that had been sending hordes of planes to the Sentani Plateau, for Anami expected to need such aircraft to make air attacks against potential American invaders at Wewak. Further, since Hollandia was so far northwest from Nadzab, Anami felt that the hordes of aircraft at Lake Sentani were perfectly safe from Allied air strikes.

Thus, the Japanese were totally unprepared for the air attack that would strike Hollandia on April 3, when 236 bombers all 111 fighters of the 5th Air Force would hit this major Japanese base. The 5th would expend more bombs and ammunition in this raid than they had used in

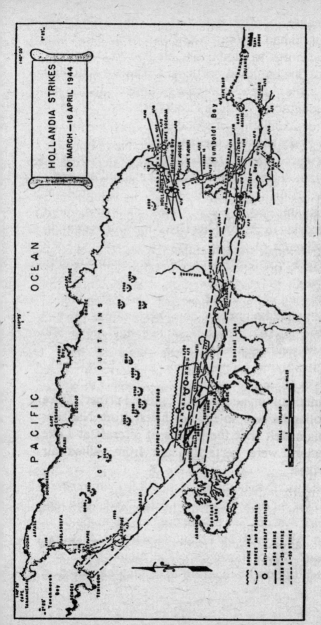

A map of 5th Air Force strikes against Hollandia before the
invasion on 22 April

any other air attack thus far during the Southwest Pacific campaign. Ironically, more than 200 Japanese planes, the most ever congested in one place, would be sitting wing tip to wing tip along the Lake Sentani runways when the Americans struck.

Just after dawn on April 3, in the sprawling Allied airbase of Port Moresby, New Guinea, 64 B-24s from the 43rd and 90th Heavy Bomb Groups rolled out of their revetment areas. Then the aircraft shattered the early morning serenity with screaming engines. They would carry 1,000 pound bombs, 492 of them, to make the initial strike on Hollandia today. By 0645 hours, all 64 Liberators were airborne and droning over the Owen Stanley Range to the Bismarck Sea beyond the north coast of New Guinea.

At Finchhaven, the 9th Squadron of the U.S. 49th Fighter Group readied P-38s at this base only 50 miles from the Japanese base at Madang. At 0730 hours, Maj. Harry Brown led 21 Lightnings over the rough taxiways toward the head of Finchhaven's single runway. By 0745 hours, the 9th Squadron commander had taken these planes aloft and within another fifteen minutes, he had rendezvoused with the 64 Liberators from Moresby. Then the 85 American planes roared westward.

The heavy bombers of the 43rd and 90th Groups would bomb the AA defenses at Tanahmerah and Humboldt Bays, and the AA pits around the airstrips on the Lake Sentani Plateau. Gen. George Kenney, the 5th Air Force commander, hoped the B-24s would knock out most of these gun positions because A-20 light bombers would be coming in after the heavies to sweep over the airfields in low level runs. The 5th Air Force CinC did not want his A-20s to speed into a wall of anti-aircraft fire.

As this first U.S. air formation droned northward, more aircraft engines shattered the quiet April 3 morning. At the major 5th Air Force base in Nadzab on the north coast of New Guinea, 48 A-20 light bombers of the 3rd Bomb Group, and the 312th Bomb Group prepared to take off from Gusap with 48 more A-20s.

In the lead Havoc of the 3rd, group commander Dick Ellis revved the twin engines of his light bomber. The colonel felt nervous, despite his full year of combat experience in the SWPA. He had participated in the astonishing victory against the Japanese armada in the Battle of the Bismarck Sea, he had been among the light bomber pilots who had made the first strike against Wewak when that Japanese base housed swarms of Zeros and countless anti-aircraft guns, and he had been on that first light bomber mission to the dreaded stronghold of Rabaul.

Ellis and his A-20 crews were not sure they could make the long 900 mile round trip to Hollandia in their light bombers. Further, the colonel worried about Japanese interceptors and the ack ack positions at Hollandia. He shuddered slightly when he squinted at the auxiliary gas tank on the A-20 next to him, just as his own Havoc carried a belly tank with extra fuel for the long flight to Hollandia. The colonel did not believe he could fly over enemy waters for more than 400 miles without detection by the enemy, and the cumbersome belly tanks would slow down his ability to manuever the A-20 against Japanese Zeros. If he got jumped so far from home and suffered damage to his plane, he doubted that he could fly all the way back to Nadzab.

The 3rd Group commander stared intently at the airstrip control tower and then picked up his radio to call his other pilots. "This is Reaper leader; Reaper leader. Please make final instrument checks."

"Okay, colonel," Maj. Ken Rosebush of the 90th Squadron answered.

Then, Dick Ellis squinted to the starboard where he could see the P-38s of the 475th Fighter Group moving over a taxiway like giant centipedes. The 475th would furnish escort for the group and Ellis at least had the satisfaction of knowing that one of the best American fighter units in the Pacific would accompany him.

When Ellis saw the yellow light from the control tower, he revved his engine once more and wheeled his plane to the head of the runway before he called his gunner, Fred Krause. "Sergeant, is everything okay back there?"

"Yes, sir," Krause answered. "Everybody's in line and moving in pairs."

"Good," Ellis said. "What about yourself?"

"I'm okay, colonel."

"Fine," the 3rd Group commander answered.

Then, the green light blinked from the control tower and Ellis reared down the runway with the wingman at his side. The two A-20s then zoomed upward and into the northern sky. Within a few moments, the other 46 Havocs of the 3rd Group had also risen into the northern sky.

Next, fighters of the 475th Group, every plane from every squadron, also reared off the runway. The 54 Lightnings, under Lt. Col. Charles MacDonald, would rendezvous with the 3rd and the 312th Group's A-20s out of Gusap over Huon Gulf for the long 450 mile flight northwestward. Once airborne, MacDonald called his pilots.

"Tighten up. When we're off the coast near Madang we'll take stations around the A-Twentys. Four thirty-first Squadron will fly in the van, Four thirty-third Squadron will fly topside to keep an eye out for bandits, and the Four thirty-second will rim around the bombers in standard pattern."

"Yes, sir, colonel," Maj. Tom McGuire of the 431st Squadron answered.

For nearly an hour, after the A-20s of the 312th Group joined, the A-20s and P-38s droned northwestward off the coast of New Guinea. As they approached the sea lanes off Wewak, the American airmen grew tense. Surely, Japanese spotters or radar operators had detected the 150 aircraft. But, no Zeros rose from the Japanese bases at Boram or But to molest the 5th Air Force planes; nor did any planes rise from

Hansa Bay to challenge the Americans. Thus, as the air formations moved far up the coast, curiosity replaced the tenseness of the 5th Air Force airmen.

Lt. Colonel McDonald called the 3rd Group commander. "Dick, what the hell's happening? We didn't see a single bandit. Are they afraid to come out?"

"Charlie," Ellis answered, "I don't think the Japs have a goddamn plane left in Boram or But. I think we've knocked out every last one of them. They don't keep many planes this far east anymore, but we may run into bandits at Hollandia itself or from Wakda-Sarmi, so you'd better stay alert."

"Dick, we'll keep bandits away, I guarantee it," MacDonald answered. "You just take care of any grounded planes we find at Hollandia."

"Will do," Ellis said.

Even as this second 5th Air Force formation droned on toward Hollandia, 70 Mitchells of the 38th and 345th Bomb Groups ignited their engines at the same sprawling U.S. base in Nadzab. These planes would follow the A-20s of the 3rd and 312th Groups to administer a second blow against grounded aircraft and installations at Hollandia.

Only a short distance away, at Nadzab's fighter strip, the 35th and 39th Squadrons of the 8th Fighter Group ignited the twin engines of their Lightnings. 38 of these fighter planes would escort the 76 Mitchell bombers.

By 0700 hours, the last formation of 5th Air

Force planes jelled into patterns over the Bismarck Sea for the long flight to Hollandia. As the U.S. airmen passed the coastline of Wewak, they too failed to meet Japanese interceptors. But the 248th Flying Regiment had too few planes at But and Boram to send out against the Americans, since the 4th Air Army had yet to send replacements.

At 0800 hours, Japanese troops at Hollandia heard the drone of planes to the southeast. At first, they thought their own aircraft might be coming in from Wewak or Aitape to join the heavy complement of 4th Air Army planes already jamming the Sentani Plateau airdromes. But then, they saw the large four engine hulks of B-24s and the twin fuselages of P-38s. Air raid sirens suddenly wailed about the Hollandia complex, all the way from Humboldt Bay to the most southerly areas near the base of the Toricelli Mountains.

Quickly, about 30 Oscar and Tony fighters of the 8th Flying Regiment under Capt. Goro Furugori roared down a runway to intercept the intruders. Furugori had seen his old 22nd Sentai air unit cut to pieces during the American assaults on Rabaul in late 1943, and he hoped he would not suffer the same fate in his new 8th Flying Regiment here at Hollandia. However, before more fighters took off, the first whistling bombs dropped from the huge bellies of the B-24s.

The bombers of the 43rd and 90th Groups displayed excellent accuracy by knocking out 26 of the 35 ack ack and artillery positions in and around the runways. They also created havoc along the shoreline.

As Furugori and his fighter pilots attempted to intercept the heavy American bombers, the 8th Flying Regiment commander and his airmen failed again as they had failed in Rabaul. Maj. Harry Brown and his 9th Squadron pilots waded into the Japanese fighter planes and the speedy, powerful Lightnings soon overwhelmed the lighter Oscar and Tony fighter planes. Brown and his pilots knocked down ten Japanese planes in moments, and even the few Japanese who broke through the P-38 screen did little damage to the powerful B-24s with their 30 caliber wing guns. The 8th Flying Regiment pilots had failed to down a single Liberator. Meanwhile, B-24 gunners themselves shot down two more of the Japanese planes.

Captain Furugori grumbled in a mixture of anger and disappointment. The Japanese commander dared not pursue the departing B-24s for he suspected that more American bombers were on the way. He had rightly guessed that the attacks on the AA positions had been designed to expose the airfields themselves. Furugori called the operations officer at 6th Air Division headquarters.

"You must send up another squadron of fighter planes at once. You should also disperse the aircraft that sit in rows along the runway, for they could be subjected to heavy air strikes."

"Yes, Honorable Furugori," a radio officer said.

But the Japanese had little time to carry out these maneuvers. They did fly off another 20 fighter planes. However, before they could move the horde of planes away from the runways, the 3rd and 312th Bomb Groups swooped across Humboldt Bay, skimmed over the jungle treetops, and then roared into the open Sentani Plateau. Col. Dick Ellis in the lead A-20 stared in astonishment at the fat targets lined up wing tip to wing tip along the Hollandia runways. He picked up his radio and called his pilots.

"Eighth and Eighty-ninth Squadrons will hit the strip designated Cyclops, Eighth on the east and Eighty-ninth on the west. Thirteenth and Ninetieth Squadrons will strike the airstrip designated Sentani, Thirteenth on the east and Ninetieth on the west."

"Okay, colonel," Major Rosebush of the 90th Squadron answered.

Then Ellis called the commander of the 312th Group. "Colonel, our Third is taking the two airstrips along the lake. Your group can hit the strip designated Hollandia Airdrome northwest of the lake."

"Okay, we'll take it."

Then, when Ellis saw the Japanese fighter planes coming towards his A-20s, he called the 475th Fighter Group commander. "Charlie, bandits are after us from two o'clock."

"We'll take care of them," MacDonald said. The 475th Group commander then led his 54 Lightnings into the Tonys and Oscars.

The Japanese, although with 40 Oscars and

Tonys airborne, could not cope with the American P-38s. More than a dozen Japanese pilots fell before the withering .50 caliber fire from the P-38 pilots. Both Charlie MacDonald and Tom McGuire got two kills themselves, while two other American pilots also downed two enemy planes.

Meanwhile, the Havocs skimmed over the runways, on both sides, unleashing heavy incendiary strafing fire from their eight nose guns that punctured rows of planes before the A-20s dropped a confetti of 100 pound parademolition bombs and clusters of 21 pound parafragmentation bombs. The assault erupted explosions, balls of fire, and thick smoke amidst the parked aircraft: Zeros, Vals, and Betty bombers. Some of the parachute explosives also destroyed buildings, vehicles, and supply dumps.

Less than a half dozen Japanese fighter planes broke through the U.S. fighter screen and they failed to down a single American light bomber.

By the time the last A-20 arced away from the three runways, they had wrecked or damaged an astounding 116 grounded planes, set more than 20 vehicles afire, disintegrated a half dozen buildings, and ignited several supply dumps. Fires raged out of control along the entire length and breadth of the Sentani Plateau. Meanwhile, P-38 pilots continued their lopsided score against Japanese interceptors, downing more Tonys and Oscars.

And the Americans were not yet finished.

By the time Ellis led the 3rd and 312th groups

away from target, the B-25s of the 38th and 345th Bomb Groups roared over the plains. 76 Mitchells now scattered more parafrags and parademos on the area, while B-25 pilots strafed everything in sight with blistering, heavy fire from ten nose guns on each plane. More explosions, fire, and smoke erupted from the battered Japanese base.

Captain Furugori now led his lacerated formations against the medium U.S. bombers. But for the third time within a half hour, the 8th Flying Regiment commander met frustration. This time, the 36 Lightnings of the 8th Fighter Group waded into the Japanese Tonys and Oscars and quickly downed six enemy planes and damaged six others, including Captain Furugori's own Tony. Luckily, Furugori belly landed his battered plane amid the raging fires along Cyclops Drome and he escaped unharmed. In turn, the 8th Fighter Group only lost two P-38s.

By the time the B-25s and their escorts left Hollandia, 36 more grounded planes had been damaged or destroyed. Meanwhile less than a dozen of the 50 Japanese fighter planes that had risen to meet the American aerial assailants had escaped the air battles unscathed.

Hollandia had suffered a serious blow. Both Gen. Masazumi Inada, commander of the 2nd Field Base in Hollandia, and Gen. Giichi Itabana, commander of the 6th Air Division, viewed the rampant destruction with disbelief. They had never seen such an astounding assault; nor could they believe that 5th Air Force could mount 300 planes for a single raid, something the Americans had never done before in the Southwest Pacific.

The next day, General Itabana sent an ironic, bittersweet message to General Teramoto, CO of the 4th Air Army. "Yesterday was the anniversary of the birthday of Emperor Meiji. We received greetings from the enemy at Hollandia which amounted to the annihilation of the Sixth Air Division in New Guinea."

Before the Japanese recovered from the disastrous April 3 raid on this major Dutch New Guinea base, the U.S. 5th Air Force continued its aerial assault on Hollandia as well as on the smaller base in Aitape. U.S. bombers hit these Japanese air fields on April 5, 8, 12, 16, and 20, causing more destruction and consternation in both regions.

Astonishingly, the Japanese interpreted the heavy, relentless air strikes on Hollandia and Aitape as a prelude to an invasion of Wewak. Gen. Korechiki Anami and Gen. Hatazo Adachi believed the Americans were attempting to neutralize Aitape and Hollandia so the 4th Air Army could not mount air strikes against an invasion of Wewak, or so the 2nd Area Forces could not organize barge convoys at Humboldt Bay to bring supplies down the coast to Wewak.

The Japanese thus worked even more fervently to complete protective measures at Wewak. Adachi soon abandoned both Medang and Hansa Bay, while he strengthened Wewak village, Boram Airdrome, and But Field. He also set up extensive defense positions, including big guns, along the Wewak coastal areas. By April 21, his 18th Army defenses had been completed.

"Let the Yankee dogs come," Adachi boasted to his staff. "We will drive them back into the sea."

But, the next day, April 22, 1944, Gen. Hatazo Adachi would get the shock of his life.

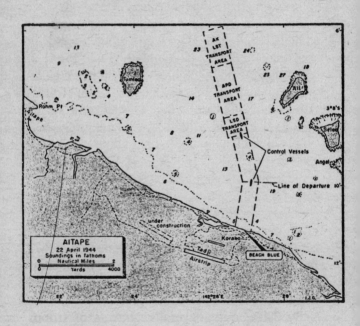

The Aitape landing operation

Chapter Four

At dawn, April 22, navy bombers of the U.S. TF 58 pulverized the airfields in the Wakde-Sarmi area, 120 miles up the coast from Hollandia, to thwart any Japanese air resistance to the American landings on Dutch New Guinea. Then, at 0650 hours, swarms of U.S. Dauntless dive bombers from carriers USS *Coral Sea* and *Manila Bay* pelted the shorelines of Tanahmerah and Humboldt Bays, shattering any Japanese defenses along the beaches. The U.S. Navy aircraft also a struck defenses inland. At 0700 hours, cruisers and destroyers of the U.S. TF 77 bombarded the landing sites on both bays, chasing off any Japanese who had survived the twin aerial-surface ship assaults.

By 0800 hours, several regiments of troops from the 24th and 41st U.S. Infantry Divisions landed on Tanahmerah Bay and Humboldt Bay respectively. The invaders met no opposition, not even a rifle shot. Most of the Japanese soldiers along the shoreline had been service troops and they simply fled before the huge

American invasion force, with its accompanying warships and swarms of aircraft from the TF 38 carriers.

The main problem for the GIs was not the enemy, but oozy swamps that lay beyond the beaches. By mid morning, the shoreline became crammed with men, supplies, ammo, and artillery, with no way to move them inland by truck. Eight days would pass before army engineers completed a causeway and road through these swamps and uphill jungles to the Sentani Plateau, fifteen miles away. Meanwhile ground troops moved inland on foot, usually in single file and carrying supplies and ammunition on their backs.

As the GIs struggled inland, they met only scattered opposition from some rear guard Japanese units. However, this minor resistance did not delay the American infantry troops and the combat aviation engineers who were right behind them. By L-day plus two, the Americans had reached the Sentani Plateau and captured, killed, or driven into the jungles any remaining Japanese troops in the area. The troops under Col. Soeman Matsuyuma could hardly resist the massive invasion, so he took the remainder of his combat forces westward over the jungle trails in the hope of reaching Wakde-Sarmi. Most of the surviving Hollandia service troops, including General Itabana, General Inada, and Captain Furugori, joined Colonel Matsuyuma in the retreat.

By L-day plus five, U.S. engineers had

repaired at least one of the airstrips and the 475th Fighter Group moved its P-38s into the captured Hollandia. By the end of April, the 9th Squadron of the 49th Fighter Group, and the A-20 bombers of the 3rd and 312th Groups had also come to Hollandia. The base was then open for business to begin a 5th Air Force assault against the Japanese at the western tip of New Guinea and even in the East Indies.

125 miles to the south, also on April 22, 1944, the American Eastern Attack Force landed on the 1200 yard stretch of beach. Six destroyers had unleashed a heavy bombardment on the flat oblong plain of Aitape. Then, Dauntless dive bombers from the TF 78.2 jeep carriers had saturated the area with bombs. An hour later, the 163rd RCT of the 41st Division and the 127th RCT of the 32nd Division had disembarked near the villages of Koroko and Wapil, only a mile from the Tadji airdromes.

The Americans had estimated the Japanese garrisons at Aitape to be about 3,500 men, of which 1,500 were combat troops. However, American intelligence had badly overestimated the number of enemy soldiers at Aitape. They later learned that only 1,000 soldiers had occupied the area, with only a half dozen field pieces and a mere 240 combat troops. As soon as the U.S. destroyers and Dauntless bombers opened on Aitape, the Japanese garrison fled the Tadji plains and disappeared into the Toricelli Mountains to the south.

The Persecution Force under Gen. Charles

Hall had thus landed at Aitape with no opposition whatever. Further, the flat plain offered much better freedom of movement than did the soggy swamps and uphill jungles of Hollandia. "We didn't expect such as easy time," Hall said later. "Within hours, we had occupied the entire Aitape area with no losses in either men or equipment."

By the end of the first day, the No. 26 Works Wing of the Australian RAAF had already begun repairs to the fighter and bomber strips, while the U.S. 114th Combat Engineers Battalion had begun construction of another airstrip on the Tadji Plantation.

"Construction and repairs went well," said Capt. William Dale, the American in charge of the 114th Engineers. "We had no problems with terrain, Japanese troops, or enemy air units."

By April 24, two days after the Aitape invasion, the RAAF 70 Wing moved 20 Beaufort light bombers and 30 P-40 fighter planes onto the Tadji airstrips. These aircraft would support troops if needed.

By the end of April, engineers had completed the installations of radar so the Allies could quickly detect any Japanese attempt to make air raids, sea attacks, or even ground assaults. Finally, General Hall set up a defensive perimeter at both the Koronal River facing the jungles to the east and along the Raihu River facing the jungles to the west. The Persecution Force commander rotated three battalions of the 163rd RCT to cover the trails from the west, while he rotated three battalions of the 127th RCT to cover the trails from the east.

"We didn't expect the Japanese to do anything," Hall said. "Hell, when we took Hollandia, all the Japanese troops ran into the mountains or onto the trails toward Wakde-Sarmi. They sure as hell weren't going to come east for a hundred twenty-five miles through the jungles to hit us at Aitape. We didn't consider any problems from the east either. Although the Japanese had a reported fifty thousand troops at Wewak, these soldiers were half starved and exhausted, with few supplies, and no planes. How the hell could they mount any counterattack through eighty miles of thick, hostile jungle?"

As the days at Aitape turned into weeks, Hall's predictions seemingly proved accurate. Except for a few minor Japanese patrols who probed the American defenses along the Koronal River, nothing happened. Further, many of these Japanese scouts were either killed, captured, or chased into the jungle, where they died of starvation or to the elements. By late June, two months after the Aitape landings, the region had settled into a quiet Allied airbase. The RAAF 40 Wing conducted routine air sorties against such Japanese as they could find in the surrounding jungles, but otherwise nothing was going on.

The same routine had developed at Hollandia where, two months after the invasion, the Americans had yet to meet Japanese group troops. But the Japanese were struggling to survive and they could hardly think of counterattacking. The Matsuyuma Force and supply troops had endured horror during their retreat through the jungles to Wakde-Sarmi. Without maps, and short of rations and supplies, the 7,000 Japanese soldiers suffered severe hardships in the hostile terrain. Hundreds died on the way from disease or starvation, and less than 50 percent of them reached Wakde-Sarmi. Of the 7,220 men who had left Hollandia, 3,400 had died on the trail, while another 600 had been captured by the Americans. Among the Japanese survivors were General Inada, General Itabana, Colonel Matsuyuma, and Captain Furugori.

The 4th Air Army, now operating out of Wakde-Sarmi, did make a few air raids on Hollandia. But their numbers were few and the 475th Group pilots under Lt. Colonel MacDonald and the 9th Squadron pilots under Maj. Harry Brown usually shot down most of the Japanese planes or drove them off. The Japanese flyers thus caused little damage to the Americans, and Hollandia soon ballooned into a major American supply, naval, and airbase. MacArthur soon spoke of new westward invasions against the Japanese.

The American occupation of Hollandia and Aitape had prompted General Anami of the 2nd Area Forces to cancel all further attempts to send the 36th or 35th Division troops into western New Guinea. He rightly held these forces in reserve for expected new invasion at-

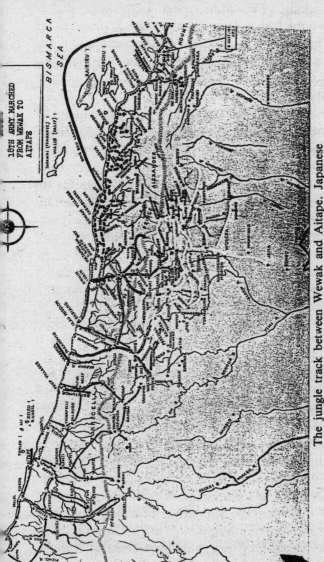

18TH ARMY MARCHED FROM WEWAK TO AITAPE

The jungle track between Wewak and Aitape. Japanese conducted amazing 80 mile march to attack Americans at Aitape

tempts further westward on New Guinea, and perhaps even into the East Indies themselves.

If the Americans had grossly underestimated the kind of opposition they might encounter in the Hollandia-Aitape operations, they had also underestimated the audacious, stubborn Gen. Hatazo Adachi.

When news of the Hollandia-Aitape invasions reached the 2nd Area Forces and 18th Army headquarters, Japanese generals and admirals were stunned. They had not prepared themselves for assaults on these New Guinea bases far up the coast, so they had offered little or no resistance. Moreover, the stalwart defenses completed at Wewak had gone for naught. Further, since the Allies controlled the skies as well as the sea lanes, the 50,000 troops of the 18th Army had been cut off and isolated by the American leap frog operations.

The 18th Army at Wewak could not move southeast since thousands of well armed American and Australian troops occupied the Saidor and Finchhaven areas. They could not evacuate Wewak since they had no means to transport this many men by sea, especially with hordes of Allied ships prowling the seas. And certainly, Adachi could not flee southward into the hostile Owen Stanley Mountains. On April 23, General Anami, from his headquarters in the Celebes, sent a message to Adachi.

"The enemy operations have left the Eighteenth Army isolated. We are in no position to help, and you are in no condition to make a counter attack. And, of course, there is no possibility now of sending air reinforcements to the Two forty-eighth Flying Regiment. Such aircraft would only become fodder for enemy air attacks. We will make every effort to evacuate by submarine as many troops as possible, especially the sick and wounded. I suggest, meanwhile, that you begin a march westward, bypassing Aitape and Hollandia, to reach the safety of Wakde-Sarmi.''

General Adachi read the message with disdain. He had no stomach for a 400 mile retreat through the jungles to reach Wadke. He believed that most of his troops would die from starvation, disease, or the elements before they reached safety. He also suspected that he would suffer battle casualties from Allied ground and air units around the Aitape and Hollandia areas.

Hundreds of stories have come out of World War II regarding the brazenness of military figures, whether they were Allied or Axis. However, perhaps no military commander of the Pacific War matched the audacity and determination of Gen. Hatazo Adachi.

Instead of following Anami's suggestion, the 18th Army commander called into conference at his Wewak headquarters his subordinate commanders: Gen. Sadahiko Miyake of the 20th Division, Col. Tokutaro Ide of the division's 80th Regiment, Col. Mitsujiro Matsumoto of the 51th Division's 78th Regiment, Col. Masahuko Nara of the 41st Division's 273rd Regiment, and Capt. Sadaaki Akamatsu of the

248th Flying Regiment.

"I have received a communication from General Anami," Adachi said. "He suggests that we make a four hundred mile retreat westward through the jungles to reach the safety of Wakde-Sarmi. We can take with us on such a retreat nothing more than supplies we must carry ourselves or on the backs of our pack horses. We would need to follow the primitive trails and then skirt the enemy positions at Hollandia and Aitape. I doubt if we could by-pass these areas without severe American air and ground attacks. It is my belief that such a retreat would be disastrous and few of us would reach Wadke."

The staff of the 18th Army only listened.

"I propose instead that we march on Aitape and recapture this base from our enemies. We would not only win thousands of tons of enemy supplies in such an effort, but we could then stage out of Aitape to recapture Hollandia."

The conferees listened in amazement to the proposal. How could they accomplish such a feat in the face of superior numbers of enemy ships, planes, guns, and men? How could they move through 80 miles of jungles with weak, tired troops and limited supplies? They would merely march to their destruction, even if they survived the exhausting march westward from Wewak. For a full minute, none of the commanders answered Adachi, but then General Miyake spoke up.

"Honorable Adachi," the 20th Division commander said, "none of us has ever questioned your courage and determination. However, is it feasible to carry out such a plan? Many of our men are feeble from lack of food and rampant disease. Our resources are badly depleted and the route between here and Aitape traverses the most hostile jungle terrain in the world."

"It is my belief," Adachi answered, "that we would find even more impossible an attempt to reach Wakde-Sarmi through five times this length of jungle. Further, the occupation of Hollandia and Aitape would make such a trek even more dangerous."

"But you are asking our troops to fight in combat, even after we have made an eighty mile trek through the rain forests," Miyake said.

"We have suffered agony during our forced retreats for more than a year; first at Buna, then at Lae, again at Finchhaven and Saidor, and now at Madang. This latest enemy operation has demoralized our troops even more. Our soldiers are disheartened and we must do something to rekindle their spirits. What could renew their pride and worth more than a victory against our enemies at Aitape?"

"The Honorable Adachi speaks wisely," Colonel Nara suddenly spoke. "We have nothing to lose if we attempt to recapture the Tadji Plantation. It is better than mildewing here at Wewak until disease and starvation claims all of us; and it is better than retreating through four hundred miles of jungle with severe losses."

"Perhaps so, colonel," Miyake said.

"The trails between here and Aitape are not the best," Adachi said, "but I believe our troops will undertake this march without complaint, even if they must carry supplies on their backs."

"I can tell you, Honorable Adachi," Nara said, "that Major Hoshimo can dismantle his heavy guns of the 41st Mountain Artillery and carry these weapons over the trail on pack horses. While your suggestion is a daring one, perhaps its very boldness would enable us to surprise and overcome our enemy."

Adachi nodded and then continued. "I will suggest to General Anami that the submarines he intends to send here for evacuation of sick and wounded should bring us supplies, food, and ammunition to carry out this plan. And," the 18th Army commander gestured, "I would not force anyone to participate in this operation. If any of you or any of the men in your commands wish to follow General Anami's suggestion for a long retreat to Wakde, you have my permission."

The officers did not answer Adachi for a full 30 seconds and then General Miyake spoke. "Honorable Adachi, please do not misinterpret my earlier doubts on this proposed plan as an unwillingness to participate. I can assure you, I will do everything possible to carry out any duties you assign me."

"I am glad to hear that, Sadahiko," Adachi grinned, "for I hope to prepare a draft for an Aitape Assault Force, and I would ask that you lead this force."

"I will do so willingly," the commander of the 20th Division said.

Adachi shuffled through some papers on the makeshift table in his tent headquarters. "My staff and I have made a survey of the arms and men available for this attack. We are badly depleted, but the Twentieth Division has all of its regiments, with perhaps three thousand healthy combat troops, one thousand men of the Twenty-sixth Mortar Battalion, and substantial service troops. By our count, the Twentieth can provide six thousand able men for combat. The Fourty-first Division has eleven thousand able men of which five thousand are honed infantry jungle fighters. We can also count on six thousand healthy combat troops from the Fifty-first Division and two thousand-five hundred men of the Forty-first Mountain Artillery Regiment. Major Hoshimo has a large number of 37mm and 75mm guns, while the Twenty-sixth Mortar Battalion has ample 51mm and 90mm mortar. Totally then, we have more than twenty thousand combat troops for this operation. We will also have at least fifteen thousand able service troops and these men will be engaged in moving supplies forward from Wewak to the front."

"What about supplies?" Colonel Ide asked.

Adachi shuffled through more papers until he pulled our another sheet. "We have enough weapons: thirteen thousand one hundred forty-two rifles, seven hundred twenty six machine guns, five hundred sixty-one grenade dischargers, thirty-two heavy mortars, twenty-two

77

light mortars, thirty-six 37mm guns, forty-two 75mm guns, and one hundred and fifty pack horses." Then the 18th Army commander squeezed his face. "Unfortunately, we have a shortage of blankets, clothing, mosquito nets and quinine. I would sadly grieve if I thought our troops suffered an unusually high incidence of malaria and dengue fever during this jungle advance on Aitape."

"Are you suggesting that we cut down the number of troops for this operation?" Colonel Ide asked.

"No," Adachi said. "I'll insist that the first submarine that comes to Wewak should carry these needed blankets, nets, clothing, and quinine as a priority."

"A good thought, Honorable Adachi," Colonel Nara said.

"We will move much of our heavy equipment by barges," Adachi said. "The barges can plot westward at night, hugging the coast, while they remain hidden during daylight hours."

"What of the others here in Wewak?" Colonel Matsumoto asked.

"Most of the remainder of our Eighteenth Army troops are quite disabled from wounds and illness. The best of them will maintain strong defenses in the Wewak area to guard against any enemy thrusts from Saidor or Finchhaven. The worst of them will be evacuated."

"That should do quite well," Colonel Matsumoto nodded.

Adachi now turned to Captain Akamatsu.

"How many airmen are healthy and able?"

"About one thousand, Honorable Adachi, of which two hundred are pilots and gunners," the 248th Flying Regiment commander answered.

"As you have heard, captain, you are not likely to get air replacements, so we must do our best with limited resources. How many serviceable aircraft do you have?"

"About twenty Mitsubishi fighters (Zeros) and perhaps a dozen Aichi dive bombers (Vals)," Captain Akamatsu said. "While we cannot use this limited number of aircraft for offensive attacks on enemy installations, we can use them for ground support. We have these Mitsubishis and Aichis well hidden in the trees at the But and Boram fields, well out of sight from enemy airmen. In fact, even while enemy air units conducted massive attacks on Hollandia and Aitape, they have made only limited attacks on Wewak. I believe the enemy is convinced that no more aircraft are in the Wewak area. So their ground forces at Aitape will be surprised indeed to find us supporting our own ground troops."

"Very good, captain," Adachi nodded. "We will call on your airmen as needed."

"Yes, Honorable Adachi."

"When do you believe we can begin this offensive?" General Miyake asked.

"I see no possibility of initiating these attacks until late June," Adachi said. "We will need to strengthen our troops with renewed exercise in jungle marches and jungle fighting, and we must build up our supplies. At the present time we have enough food and other needs to last us until August, perhaps September at the latest. We will need supplies at an accelerated pace if we are to march into combat instead of sitting idly here in Wewak."

"But will not the Americans at Aitape be unusually strong by then?" General Miyake asked.

"The contrary may be true," Adachi said. "The longer they sit in Aitape with no opposition, the more they will be convinced that no attack is forthcoming. I suspect that by the end of June, they will have no more than a regiment of troops in the area, plus supply and service troops."

Adachi paused, studied the papers in front of him, and then continued. "We will send out small units to continually probe the enemy lines at Aitape. We will thus know the enemy's disposition at all times. No unit larger than squad size will move into any area. We want the Americans to believe we are doing nothing more than scouting them. The more confident they become, the more we can surprise and defeat this enemy."

"I agree, general," Colonel Nara said.

"The Second Battalion of the Eightieth Regiment is now resting at Yakamul, fifty miles to the north," Colonel Ide siad. "Lt. Colonel Tsuji has informed me that the batalion has made excellent progress and that his men are in good spirits. What should Tsuji do now that the enemy has occupied Aitape and Hollandia?"

"You will ask Lt. Colonel Tsuji to remain encamped at Yakamul and supply the scouting parties of which I mentioned," Adachi gestured. "His units can reconnoiter the American positions west of the Driniumor River on a daily basis. By the time we have moved our army into position for the attack on Aitape, Lt. Colonel Tsuji should have complete information on the deployment and strength of enemy troops."

"Lt. Colonel Tsuji is a capable commander," General Miyake said, "and his men of the Second Battalion are good soldiers. They will carry out instructions with unquestioned haste and efficiency."

"Good," Adachi said. "Are there any more questions?" When no one answered, the 18th Army commander continued. "You will return to your units and begin training exercises at once. Meanwhile, I will contact the Honorable Anami and inform him of our decision to recapture Aitape. I will ask that he send us as many supplies as possible."

The next day, when Gen. Korechika Anami got the decoded message from Wewak, the 2nd Area Forces commander was stunned by Adachi's ambitious plan. Anami's first instinct was to chastise the 18th Army commander and to order Adachi and his thousands of troops to begin the march to Wakde, while submarines came to Wewak to evacuate the most critically sick and wounded of the 18th Army. But, Anami hesitated until he recovered from the shock. By afternoon, he called his 2nd Area Forces staff to a meeting at his headquarters in

Manado, Celebes. When he explained Adachi's plans, the officers reacted with awe as well as surprise.

"And have the commanders and troops of the Eighteenth Army agreed to this intrepid proposal?" General Teramoto of the 4th Air Army asked.

Anami grinned. "General Adachi offered every soldier in his command the opportunity to forsake this astounding operation, and to follow my suggestion for withdrawing to Wakde-Sarmi. Not a single officer or man in the Eighteenth Army refused to follow the Honorable Adachi."

General Teramoto also grinned and then spoke to Anami. "May I suggest that we permit General Adachi to attempt this remarkable feat? Its very boldness may result in success. What Allied commander would expect such an effort? Even if the Eighteenth Army only recaptures Aitape and not Hollandia, such a victory would bring consternation to the Americans."

"My own thoughts exactly," Anami nodded. Then he sighed. "We of the Second Area Forces must do everything possible to aid General Adachi in this endeavor. We must assign at least a squadron of submarines to carry as many provisions as possible to Wewak and to evacuate the mostly badly injured and sick. We will also furnish whatever barges we can for the movement of supplies and arms toward Aitape." He turned to an aide. "You will notify Admiral Endo at once that he must use as many submarines and barges as possible to aid the Honorable Adachi."

"Yes, general," the aide said.

For the next two months, Adachi's commanders worked hard with the troops at Wewak to ready them for the 80 mile advance through the jungles for the recapture of Aitape. 9th Fleet submarines continually brought supplies to Wewak, while barges moving at night carried supplies up to Yakamul. Meanwhile, Tsuji's patrols did an excellent job of reconnoitering American defenses along the Koronal River. Not only did these scouting parties bring back accurate information, but they had also convinced the Americans that the Japanese had planned nothing more for Aitape than snooping missions. General Hall, the U.S. Persecution Force commander, grew more complacent: the Japanese would never attack Aitape.

By late June, every commander from General MacArthur on down expected the trapped 18th Army to evacuate Wewak by barge or submarine, or to attempt a long withdrawal through the jungles to western New Guinea as the thousands of troops under General Inada had done from Hollandia.

Adachi suffered only one minor setback to his plans. His officers had needed a little more time than expected to ready the combat troops, and Admiral Endo's submarines had taken more time than expected to bring needed supplies to Wewak. The 18th Army commander merely postponed the date of his Aitape assault to July 10, 1944.

In late June, Lt. Colonel Masanasobu Tsuji

informed 18th Army headquarters that he now had an excellent picture of the American defenses east of Aitape. He spoke of the American complacency concerning possible Japanese attacks. Tsuji suggested that Adachi could strike the Americans with complete surprise, especially since the Japanese could hide massive troops movements in the dense, remote jungles between Wewak and Aitape.

But, uncannily, a U.S. Army sergeant, an infantry squad leader, would become suspicious of the Japanese plans. The non-com, who had made regular routine patrols west of the Koronal River, had concluded that the Japanese were driving northwestward from Wewak with heavy forces. The sergeant would wade through red tape to reach General Hall himself and convince the Persecution Force commander that the Japanese were preparing for a massive attack on Aitape.

Chapter Five

The 32nd U.S. Infantry Division, the Red Arrows, had been among the most capable jungle fighters in the Southwest Pacific. They had wiped out the Japanese at Buna, in the first major Allied victory in the Pacific. They had overrun the enemy at Finchhaven, administering heavy losses to the Japanese, they had chased the Japanese out of Saidor, again with heavy losses. The Red Arrows had so badly mauled the 18th Army during the past 1½ years in New Guinea, that General Adachi had referred to the 32nd Division infantrymen as Jungle Lizards. The 32nd dogfaces had worn this name as a badge of pride.

In truth, the 32nd GIs had indeed become adept jungle lizards in the Pacific. Among these dogfaces was Sgt. Ed Madcliff, a handsome man with a beanpole build. He had joined the 32nd Red Arrow Division in 1940 at Madison, Wisconsin, where the 32nd had been a national guard unit in the upper midwest area. When the Red Arrows moved to Camp Beauregard, Louisiana, for training a year later, Madcliff was made corporal and an assistant squad leader. By the time the division sailed for Australia in early 1942, Madcliff had reached the rank of sergeant. New members to the 32nd had looked on him with a sense of admiration because of his intelligence and leadership qualities.

During the Papuan campaign in the fall of 1942, Madcliff had offered an excellent example of his uncanny instinct for detecting hidden Japanese snipers and defenses. Near the Golden River, he had stopped his squad for no apparent reason and one of his men had frowned.

"I don't see nothin'; what are we waitin' for?"

"The bastards are right up ahead," Madcliff had answered. The discerning squad leader had noticed sunlight twinkling through the gnarled tree branches. There had been no breeze and the birds were gone. Something was disturbing the leaves and branches. Madcliff had retired his patrol for 30 yards and then unleashed a dozen rounds of 60mm mortar fire into the trees. Moments later, when the GIs advanced again, the squad found 20 dead Japanese snipers.

Since that day in New Guinea's highland jungles, no one had ever again questioned Sergeant Madcliff's remarkable instinct. The incident, in fact, had prompted the division's 127th Regimental commander to use the Madison, Wisconsin, native as a reconnaissance patrol leader. Madcliff had not failed his colonel. Without detection by the enemy, he had continually discovered Japanese positions—during the battle for Buna and the Battle for Saidor. Now, at Aitape in June of 1944, with the rank of staff sergeant, Madcliff still led reconnaissance patrols into the deep, eerie New Guinea jungles.

Col. Merle Howe, Commander of the 32nd Division's 127th Regiment had begun patrols east of the Nigia River as soon as his unit arrived in Aitape in June of 1944 to relieve the 163rd RCT.

For several weeks, infantry patrols had probed the jungle, sometimes as far east as the Driniumor River. On June 24, Sgt. Ed Madcliff was leading a squad of twelve men through the dense brakes. For two days the patrol had tramped through deep mud, murky swamps, dense trees, and jungle brush. They had lived on K rations, slept in pup tents, and fought insects and leeches. The men had tired of the gloomy ghost forests, for they had not seen a sign of the enemy in the eerie terrain. Finally, when they crossed the Driniumor and continued eastward, a rifle man turned to his squad leader.

"Jesus, sarge, how far are we goin' in this fuckin' jungle?"

"We'll move until we find out what those yellow son's a bitches are up to," Madcliff barked.

"They're not up to a goddamn thing," the private answered. "All we seen was a couple of small patrols and the bastards ran off when we came close to them. Christ, they've had dogfaces wandering through this asshole forest for more than two months and nobody ever seen nothin' but a few Japs wonderin' around doin' nothin', just like us."

"We'll stay out for a few more days."

"A few more days!" the private gasped. "We've already crossed two rivers. We're so goddam far east, I don't think we can find our way back to Tadji. Christ, if we keep goin' we'll be in Wewak."

"We'll go as far as the Harech River," Madcliff said.

The men of the squad grumbled but they continued on, swatting away insects of every description that flitted about their perspiring bodies, picking off leeches that tried to dig through their leggings to suck blood from their skin, and squirming uncomfortably to mitigate the itching sweat on their bodies.

By mid morning the next day, June 25, when the squad reached the Harech, Madcliff stiffened. He heard voices and he detected movements across the shallow, fifty foot wide stream. "I think there's a bunch 'a the bastards on the other side," he whispered to his corporal. "We'll go upstream a ways, cross the river, and try to hit 'em from behind."

The corporal did not answer. He knew that Madcliff would ignore any protest. The twelve GIs then waded carefully and quietly across the Harech River some 200 yards to the south. Then Madcliff led the soldiers through the jungle in the direction of the chattering voices. Soon the patrol leader spotted a horde of Japanese troops, forty or fifty of them. Madcliff gestured his men to cover and he then studied the enemy soldiers through binoculars. The Japanese were stowing packs on their backs, apparently preparing to march out of the jungle clearing. The enemy soldiers were also loading dismantled mortars, light artillery, and other supplies on the backs of pack animals. The sergeant turned to his corporal.

"Joe, they're getting ready to move in force. Take a look."

The corporal also looked at the Japanese activities through field glasses and he then squeezed his face. "Goddamn it, Ed," he whispered. "We never seen pack animals before on any of these patrols."

The corporal as well as Ed Madcliff had come to understand the Japanese routine. The enemy always traveled lightly and in small groups when they were simply on reconnaissance patrols. They rarely carried heavy burdens and certainly they did not lead pack animals on patrols. No, they used laden mules or horses, especially with mortar and artillery burdens, only when they moved forward to engage in offensive battles. The Japanese had done so at Buna, at Finchhaven, and at Saidor, when they had tried to counterattack.

"What are you gonna do, Ed?"

"Take 'em out," Madcliff said.

"What?" the corporal hissed. "They got us outnumbered three or four to one."

"But they don't know we're here," Madcliff

said. "We'll take 'em from two sides before they know what hit 'em."

Madcliff was sure he would catch the Japanese by surprise for his was the first U.S. patrol to come this far east from Aitape. The American squad sergeant was anxious to get into the Japanese camp because he believed he might come up with some vital information. And in truth, Tsuji's patrol leaders, staging out of Yakamul a few miles to the east, always carried maps and other documents with them.

Madcliff split his men into two groups. "Joe, I'll wait ten minutes. Check your watch. At 1030 hours we'll open on them from both flanks. Make every shot count."

"Okay, Ed," the corporal said.

Madcliff then moved slowly forward with his five men while the corporal stalked cautiously through the underbrush to reach the north flank of the enemy camp. By 1028 hours, both groups had reached good positions to hit the Japanese, who continued with nonchalant innocence their routine chores of storing gear and supplies. At 1030 hours, Madcliff dropped his arm.

Simultaneously, from both flanks, the Americans opened with a deadly barrage of fire from BAR's, bazookas, tommy guns, and rifles. The sudden fusillade caught the Japanese totally off guard in their jungle clearing and within the first moments, more than half of them fell dead or wounded. And even as the Nippon troops attempted to scatter, Madcliff and his men sent thumping bazooka shells and hand grenades into their midst. More of the Japanese fell from exploding shrapnel.

"Hoda! Hoda!" the Japanese officer in charge shouted anxiously. He gestured furiously to his men, trying to get them to safety.

Madcliff scrupulously noted the officer and the American sergeant aimed a rifle carefully before he squeezed the trigger. The bullet caught the Japanese captain squarely in the neck. The officer gasped once and then fell to the ground. A second soldier, a sergeant, quickly took over command. Madcliff aimed his rifle again and shot this man dead with a bullet through the temple.

Now leaderless, the surviving Japanese troops stampeded in several directions. Some rushed into the river where in the open they became fodder for American guns. Others ran headlong to the north or south, squarely into the point blank fire of BARs and tommy guns. A few lucky ones ran to the east to escape the massacre. Less than five minutes after the barrage began, the patch of jungle reverted to an eerie silence, with a mist of gun smoke hovering above the bloody clearing like an eerie fog.

"Let's go," Madcliff cried, "and stay alert."

The twelve GIs moved carefully into the clearing and pointed their weapons at the distorted, fallen bodies of enemy troops. Blood soaked the ground, smeared the gray uniforms of the dead, or flowed from their startled faces. Occasionally, one of the GIs unleashed a stream of bullets on a downed Nippon soldier who seemed to move. The Americans knew that wounded and dying Japanese often tossed grenades or fired guns point blank at their attackers.

Quickly, Madcliff and his men searched the bodies of the dead enemy soldiers, especially the captain and sergeant, to extract maps and other papers. The Americans also searched through the packs on the backs of the slain enemy or through the bundles on the backs of horses. When Madcliff was satisfied that he had probably found all he could, the sergeant turned to his men.

"Okay, let's get the hell out of here. We'll be in for a tough day because nobody stops until we cross the Nigia River. I don't care if we have to march all night. I want to reach our lines within the next twenty-four hours."

"Chirst, sarge, that's twenty-five miles. We'll drop of exhaustion before we reach our perimeter."

"We'll die from Japanese bullets if we don't," Madcliff answered. "A few of those bastards got away and I suspect their main body is at Yakamul, only a few miles east. When their commander finds out what happened here, he'll likely send a whole goddamn battalion after us."

The GIs could not disagree, for in previous jungle battles, they had seen the Japanese often react swiftly after a severe loss. So, the GIs straightened resolutely and began a long, hard trek through the jungle. They crossed the Harech River and continued on, sweating and aching as they plodded through thick brush. Soon, their backs pained, their legs grew numb, and their bodies wilted. But still Madcliff drove the GIs on, stopping only for ten minute breaks every hour. During the torturous march, their feet became sore and their ankles swelled. They eventually crossed the Niumen Creek and they finally reached the Driniumor River. They had made over ten miles in less than seven hours.

"G-Goddamn, Ed," the corporal said. "We can't go no further. Can't we rest 'til morning?"

Madcliff squinted into the dark green jungle behind him. He did not see or hear anything, but he felt sure the enemy was in pursuit. He looked at his corporal and shook his head. "We can't stop, Joe. The men can wash in the river and eat some chow. Maybe we'll rest for an hour, but no more."

"Jesus, it'll be dark in an hour."

"Too bad," the sergeant answered. "We're pretty familiar with these trails going west from the Driniumor here. We'll just follow them."

The men protested. They were nearly exhausted, quite sore, and sadly weak. They wanted to camp on the west bank of the Driniumor River for the night. The water relieved the pain to some degree, but had hardly refreshed them. Still, at sunset, the patrol moved on again with men grumbling and cursing their sergeant.

However, Sgt. Ed Madcliff had wisely ignored the complaints of his men. Less than a half hour after he and his squad had all but wiped out the

Japanese force, two lucky Nippon escapees had reached Lt. Colonel Tsuji's headquarters in Wakamul to report the massacre. Like Madcliff, the Lt. Colonel had been a jungle fighter for many months and he rightly guessed that the American assassins had probably discovered the truth—the Japanese were planning an assault in force against Aitape. Tsuji knew that a U.S. patrol with a smart, experienced leader would understand that pack animals, mortar, and artillery were clues to some offensive operation.

Tsuji quickly summoned one of his company commanders and ordered him to take a hundred men westward to run down the American force. "You must find and kill them before they return to their position west of the Nigia River. They must be very tired if they came as far as the Herach River and they will need to rest somewhere for the night, perhaps at Niumen Creek, and surely no further west than the Driniumor River. If you move swiftly with little rest, you can overtake them."

"Yes, Honorable Tsuji," the captain said.

But, Madcliff's foresight had thwarted the Japanese. The 100 soldiers would not catch the dozen GIs. By noon, the Japanese captain had reached the ambush site, where he stopped only long enough to survey the carnage with sour distaste. He left a burial party of ten men behind and he then crossed the Harech with his remaining troops to move swiftly up the trail, crossing Niuman Creek and finally reaching the Driniumor River well after dark. But the Japanese were still two hours behind Madcliff and his squad.

"The enemy is no doubt encamped a short distance on the west side of the river," the captain said. "We will send out scouts to find them and then we will attack these Americans after dark."

"Yes, honorable captain."

The recon patrol moved nearly three miles up the trail west of the Driniumor River without finding a sign of the Americans, except for discarded K-ration tins and cardboard boxes. The scouts rightly concluded that the Americans had not stopped for the night, but had continued on without rest. When these reconnoiters returned to the Japanese encampment and reported, the captain scowled in anger.

"Bakyara!" he cursed. "The leader of the enemy unit has acted wisely. He no doubt suspected that we would pursue him with a large force and he cleverly pushed his men on."

"Shall we continue westward, captain? We can reach the bank of the Nigia River sometime after midnight."

"No," the captain shook his head. "We cannot overtake these Americans now, and we dare not expose a large force such as ours to the enemy on the Nigia River. We will camp here on the Driniumor River and return to Wakamul in the morning." The officer sighed. "Perhaps this small American force merely slew our soldiers and fled. They may not be aware of our plan to recapture Aitape."

"Yes, captain."

However, Ed Madcliff had recovered important papers from the dead Japanese. The American patrol leader could not read Japanese, but when he studied the maps and papers, he interpreted the lines and markings on the maps as apparent attack routes in a thrust across the Nigia River to overrun the Tadji airdromes.

Madcliff's patrol, utterly spent, finally reached the Nigia River some two hours after midnight. The men quickly feel asleep and Madcliff himself decided to wait until morning before making his report.

After breakfast, at about 0700 hours, June 26, the lanky sergeant called on Capt. Leonard Lowry, his I Company commander. Lowry was surprised to see his non-com because he had not expected Madcliff back for another day or two. The captain knew the patrol had gone far to the east in one of the longest probes yet since the Americans landed at Aitape in April.

"They're on the move, sir," Madcliff told Lowry.

"You mean in force?"

"Yes, sir," Madcliff answered.

"We've had all kinds of fragmentary data to suggest that," Lowry conceded, "reports from reconn planes, word from natives, interrogation of prisoners, and unusually heavy barge movements up the coast. But none of the information is really absolute, so General Hall isn't convinced the Japanese will try to move a half starved army through eighty miles of jungle to hit us."

"They're using pack mules and loading them with mortar and artillery, sir," Madcliff said. "That means an offensive operation."

"Maybe, but that won't be enough to sway the general."

"We also have these," Madcliff said, handing Captain Lowry the maps and papers the sergeant and his men had taken from the slain Japanese.

When the I Company commander scanned the documents, his eyes widened. "Christ, Ed, you *do* have something here. I'll take this stuff to Colonel Howe. Maybe you ought to come along with me."

"Yes, sir."

Captain Lowry first saw his own 3rd Battalion commander. Lt. Col. Ed Block. Block listened to Madcliff, looked at the captured maps and papers, and then nodded. "We've got something solid here this time. Let's see Howe."

When the commander of the 127th Infantry Regiment listened to Sergeant Madcliff and scanned the documents, he too was impressed. Howe grinned at Madcliff and then turned to Captain Lowry. "If any man in this regiment can find the truth, it's Madcliff here. There's no doubt—from what the sergeant observed and from these papers, the enemy is on the move. I'm goddamn glad that Madcliff went all the way to the Harech."

By noon, Colonel Howe met with Gen. Charles Hall and Gen. William Gill, the 32nd Infantry Division commander. Hall quickly ordered G-2 personnel to study the captured documents and by mid afternoon, the Persecution Force commander received a vital report. The maps, the G-2 men said, were plans for a three pronged drive across the Nigia River. Two columns would overrun the Tadji airdromes, while the third would overrun the Aitape coastal area. A translation of the papers revealed that the Japanese intended to make an assault with 20,000 men, with another 10,000 in reserve. Finally, the paper hinted that these assaults against the American perimeters would take place during the first or second week of July.

Neither Hall nor Gill questioned the information, for they knew that Japanese officers always carried maps and papers for military operations. General Gill had often found such papers during the 32nd Infantry operations at Saidor. Further, Gill suspected that Sergeant Madcliff and his patrol may have attacked a vanguard force that was heading for the Driniumor to set up a Japanese defense line. The 32nd commander suggested that Hall contact Gen. Walter Krueger, the 6th Army commander, and Hall concurred.

Krueger listened to Hall and then shook his head. "Goddamn, would they be that brazen? I suspected the 18th Army might be establishing positions along the coast west of Wewak, but I thought they were doing this to protect their trapped army while they marched north to Wakde-Sarmi in retreat. I would have guessed they were trying to reach the rest of the 2nd Army in western New Guinea. But an attack on

Aitape? That's incredible!''

"The information is solid, Walt,'' Hall said. "The Japanese Twentieth Division has strong units in the Marabian area and maybe a full battalion as far west as Wakamul. The captured documents also indicate that the Twentieth and Forty-first Divisions are massing alone the Dandriwad River. And of course, we have the maps. It appears they definitely intend to make a triple thrust to overrun Aitape.''

"It sure looks like it,'' Krueger nodded. "Okay, we'll meet with MacArthur.''

The next day, Krueger and Hall met with MacArthur at Lae, the ADVON SWPA headquarters in eastern New Guinea. When Hall explained what he had learned and showed the CinC of the Southwest Pacific forces the maps, MacArthur pursed his lips. "These documents pretty well prove that they'll hit our perimeters sometime in July,'' Hall said. "They want to overrun Aitape and take back Tadji. But, even if they can't, they'd tie us up quite badly and we'd have to postpone any more offensive operations in western New Guinea.''

"I thought they'd written off the Eighteenth Army,'' MacArthur said, "but I think these documents are accurate. I suppose they have nothing to lose if they try to recapture Aitape. However, I'd like some verification. On the next air strike against Wewak, I want the airmen to study the area carefully. In fact, we could even feign damage to a couple of aircraft so they can sputter and stall around Yakamul and the

Dandriwad River for a good look. If they spot any large enemy ground units in that area, we'll move at once."

"Good enough, sir," Hall answered the SWPA CinC.

That very afternoon, twelve A-20s from the 3rd Bomb Group's 90th Squadron under Maj. Ken Rosebush made a low level bombing run on Wewak to chop up runways and destroy vehicles. The pilots and gunners also made close observations of activities around the Japanese base. On the way back to Hollandia, Rosebush and his wingman feigned damage and they loitered low around both Yakamul and the Dandriwad River. While pilots observed, the A-20 gunners took photos. By late afternoon, the developed pictures and pilot reports confirmed the suspicions—Japanese troops were massing at Wewak, on the Dandriwad, and at Wakamul.

"That does it," MacArthur barked. "We'll reinforce Aitape."

The CinC quickly found troopships to send the 112th Cavalry Regiment to Aitape along with the 129th Field Artillery who would move their big guns to the west banks of the Koronal and X-ray Rivers, east of the Tadji airdromes. The Australian 70 Wing increased its aircraft strength at Tadji with another squadron of Beaufort light bombers and P-40 fighters. The 5th Air Force also ordered the 3rd and 312th Bomb Groups at Hollandia to remain on full alert.

MacArthur had also ordered the 124 RCT to move to Aitape as a reserve unit to use if and when needed.

General Hall and General Gill then sent up a six mile defense line far to the east at the Drinimor River. The forces included the 3rd Battalion of the 127th Infantry Regiment and the 1st Battalion of the 128th Infantry Regiment, both from the 32nd Division. The line also included the 112th Cavalry Regiment companies on the south. Meanwhile, other combat battalions of these three regiments set up defenses along the Koronal and X-ray Rivers: those of the 128th on the north, those of the 127th in the center, and those of the 112th in the south. In the event the Japanese broke through the Driniumor River defenses, and withdrawal became necessary, the Americans could retire to these secondary defenses with minimum confusion.

General Hall's final order was quite ominous and explicit. "Without instructions, no unit is to retreat from the Driniumor River in the face of the enemy."

By July 4, the Americans had completed defenses at Aitape. Combat infantry troops had dug into trench lines on the banks of the Driniumor. The GIs aimed machine guns, mortar tubes, and light artillery barrels at the opposite bank of the river. Aussie light bombers and fighter planes, about sixty aircraft in all, stood on full alert at the Tadji airfields, bomb bays and wings guns loaded. The big 155mm and

205mm cannon stood poised on the banks of the Nigia River to hit Japanese troops should the enemy break through both the Driniumor and secondary defenses. Even destroyers from Admiral Barney's TF 77 stood offshore to lambaste enemy troops with 5'' shells.

On July 5, Percussion Force headquarters in Aitape got a new message from a reconnaissance patrol. "Westward movement of strong enemy patrols noted about the Niumen Creek. Intense activities indicate that a strong outpost will be established to cover assembly of main body in preparation for attack."

When Gen. Charles Hall got the report, he scowled. "Son of a bitch! They *are* coming."

"We'll be ready for them, sir," an aide said.

"I want a directive sent to all units: 'Enemy assault against the Driniumor River defenses can be expected at any day. Remain on full alert.' Get that out at once, major."

"Yes, sir," the aide said.

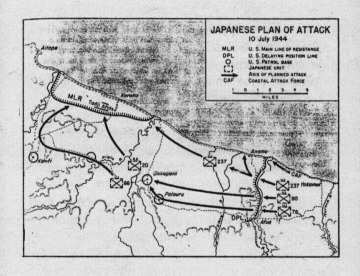

Japanese planned a three pronged attack on Aitape to capture Tadji airdromes

Chapter Six

Two weeks earlier, on June 21, before the 18th Army began its long march to Aitape, General Adachi had called his commanders together to issue final plans for an attack on the Americans.

"Lieutenant Tsuji has fully secured the Yakamul area," Adachi told his commanders, "and we may now send a strong, well armed unit to Niumen Creek to secure positions on the east bank. We will then move our troops northward to begin this offensive against Aitape." He gestured to an aide who handed out sheets of papers and maps to the commanders.

"Please study the maps to understand the suggested maneuvers," the 18th Army commander said. "You can see that we have proposed a three pronged attack. Three regiments will cross the Driniumor River and advance in this triple column toward the enemy defenses on the Nigia River. Colonel Matsumoto's Seventy-eighth Regiment will attack on the southern front, through Afua, across the X-ray River, over the

Palauru Track, and into the enemy's lower perimeter. Once across the Nigia River, these troops will make a wide sweep over jungle trails and overrun the areas on the west lateral of the enemy's Aitape positions. Do you understand, colonel?"

"Yes, Honorable Adachi," Matsumoto answered.

Adachi then looked at Tokutaro Ide. "You can see from the map, colonel, that your Eightieth Regiment will cross the Driniumor River in the center, ford the X-ray River, and drive straight for Chinapelli. Once you have secured this village, you will continue to the Nigia River, overrun any defenders on the other side, and drive directly to the Tadji airfields."

"I see, general," Colonel Ide said.

The 18th Army commander next looked at Masahuko Nara. "Your part in this plan may be quite dangerous, colonel, for the Two thirty-seventh Regiment must advance along the coastal trails. Enemy warships offshore may bombard your troops. But if you are careful, you might conceal your men during the daylight hours."

"My troops have learned well the art of camouflage, Honorable Adachi, especially in the jungle."

"Good," Adachi nodded. "Your regiment has been designated the Coastal Force since you will have with you most of the Forty-first Mountain Artillery Battalion. The big guns can move most easily over the coastal trails, so I have assigned Major Hoshimo's unit to your force."

"Fine," Colonel Nara said.

"You will cross the Driniumor River in the coastal area and seize the village of Anamo. You will then cross the Koronal River and continue along the coastal trails to the mouth of the Nigia River. Once across, you will advance your troops to Korako, the main enemy headquarters on the seashore of Aitape."

The 237th Infantry commander nodded.

"You can understand from these charts," Adachi gestured, "that the three pronged drive is designed to assail the enemy from all directions. If we are successful, we will overrun and destroy the Allied troops in the Aitape region. At worst, they will be driven into the sea." The general paused and then scanned his officers. "After you have carefully read your duties in this offensive, you can explain to your subordinates their parts in this endeavor. I would like to start moving our troops westward by sometime tomorrow."

"Yes, Honorable Adachi," Colonel Ide said.

The 18th Army commander now looked at General Miyake. "Does the plan meet with your approval, Sadahiko?"

"It is well conceived," the 20th Division commander answered.

"Is there any change that you think necessary?"

"No," Miyake gestured, "the plan is fine."

"I would ask that you assume command of this Aitape Assault Force and direct the tactical aspect of this operation in the field."

"I shall do so," Miyake said. "I will meet with the operational commanders in the morning, before we begin the movement of troops. May I suggest, Hatazo, that we send copies of these maps and plans at once to Lt. Colonel Tsuji at Wakamul, perhaps by swift couriers. Since his battalion is already far to the west, he can supply the units for establishing the perimeters on the banks of Niumen Creek."

"An excellent idea, Sadahiko," Adachi grinned.

Within a day, swift runners from the 18th Army hurried through the jungles to deliver copies of maps, papers, and orders to Lt. Col. Masanasobu Tsuji at Yakamul. The 2nd Battalion commander read the operational plans with relish, for nothing could please the jungle fighter more than a new offensive.

Tsuji was among the most agressive and harsh combat officers in the Japanese army. He had always demanded complete discipline among his men and an unwavering obedience to his orders. He had begun his career as a young lieutenant during the fighting in China some five years ago, and he had been among the most successful small unit leaders in the campaign. However, he had also shown an utter disregard for those he conquered, whether soldiers or civilians. Tsuji had treated the vanquished with unusual harshness and stern authority. He had shot without hesitation any Chinos who had balked at his commands.

By the beginning of World War II, Tsuji had risen to the rank of captain in charge of a company. He had been with General Yamashita in the Malaysian campaign and he had emulated the Tiger of Malaya with his fierceness and determination. Tsuji had run roughshod over the Burmese, Malaysians, and Vietnamese in the Southeast Asia fighting. He had shown little sympathy or patience to those he captured. By the time the Japanese had won Singapore, Tsuji had risen to an assistant battalion commander with the rank of major.

For more than a year, Tsuji had continued leading jungle fighters, especially in the New Guinea war. By early 1944, he had been promoted again and placed in charge of a battalion. By now, the end of June in 1944, the lt. colonel was awaiting another promotion and the command of a regiment. If he could succeed in this responsibility to establish a strong perimeter on Niumen Creek against American patrols, he might accelerate his rise to full colonel.

As soon as he got the orders from Wewak, Tsuji called on one of his company commanders. "You will take a platoon of men and construct a defense position on Niumen Creek, west of the Harech River, as suggested by Colonel Ide. The Eighteenth Army will begin sending combat troops westward in a day or two and we will have the obligation of securing the jungle trails for these movements."

"I will not fail, colonel," the captain answered.

"Here are copies of the plan of attack along with maps for you and your chief non-commissioned officer," Tsuji continued. "You and your sergeant should read the material carefully so you are fully acquainted with our strategy. I would also suggest that you take some mortar and light artillery along. You can dismantle these heavier weapons and carry them on pack animals."

"Yes, colonel."

"You may spend the remainder of this day and the early morning in preparing your expedition. You should reach Niumen Creek sometime tommorow afternoon and perhaps your defenses will be in place by evening."

"We will do so," the captain promised.

Throughout the rest of the day, the officer readied 44 men, two tons of supplies, four small 51mm mortars, and two 37mm artillery pieces. By sun up the next morning, the captain was ready. He only allowed his men tea before he left the Yakamul encampment, promising to stop on the banks of the Harech River for a full breakfast. By mid-morning, the Japanese troops had reached a jungle clearing on the banks of the river and the solidiers had stopped to prepare and eat a good breakfast of rice, canned fish, hard biscuits, and tea. The troops had received priority rations because of their duty to move swiftly to Niumen Creek.

Unfortunately for the Japanese, they had not considered the possibility of American patrols in the area. They were certain that no U.S. scouting parties would venture beyond the Driniumer River, some ten miles to the west. So they made no provision to maintain posted sentinels during breakfast and rest break; nor did they make any effort to remain vigilantly quiet. Ironically, the Japanese had chosen the wrong time and place for a break since Sgt. Ed Madcliff and his patrol had reached the same area of the Harech River during the same hour.

By late morning of June 27, Madcliff and his GIs had slaughtered the Japanese captain and most of his troops. The Americans had then extracted the maps and documents that revealed the Japanese plans for the attack on Aitape.

As soon as the report of the massacre on the Harech River reached Wakamul, Tsuji sent a 100 man force after the Americans, the force that had failed to catch up to Madcliff and his American patrol. Tsuji then, had sent out a new party to set up defenses on the Niumen Creek. This follow up unit maintained a careful watch during their activities and they reached the stream without incident.

When General Adachi learned of the tragedy on the Harech River, he raged in fury. He cursed the lack of alertness against enemy patrols and he berated Lt. Colonel Tsuji and the slain captain for alleged shortsightedness. After he calmed down, the 18th Army commander ordered an acceleration of troop movements northward and by July 5, the entire 20,000 men were threading forward over the narrow jungle trails.

The July 5 message to Percussion Force headquarters from the American reconnaissance patrol proved quite accurate. The Japanese were indeed on the march. Their nearly 20,000 combat troops, with attached artillery and supply troops, were plodding over the jungle trails towards Aitape. 18th Army units were strung out in an almost continuous line from Wewak to the east banks of Niumen Creek, a mere eight miles from the Driniumor River. The advance Japanese company of men had completed its strong defenses on the creek to protect the jungle trails to the east.

However, by this same July 5 date, American troops were firmly entrenched far to the east in defense positions along the Driniumor River. Secondary American defenses were also along the X-ray and Koronal Rivers.

Reports of the huge Japanese troop movements east of the Driniumor had filtered not only into Aitape but throughout the remainder of the Southwest Pacific. As the GIs at Aitape prepared their defenses, they grew tense. The Allies enjoyed superior numbers in men, arms, air units, and naval forces. But the Japanese advantage lay in their determination, steadfastness, and desperation. Adachi had whipped his troops into a frenzy and every man in the 18th Army had worked himself into a fanatic delirium, disregarding the odds. The Japanese needed a victory badly and they saw an opportunity for such a triumph at Aitape.

Despite the hurried American presence on the

Driniumor, General Adachi never wavered from his plan. He told General Miyake that his Aitape Assault Force would simply need to engage the Americans on the Driniumor, overrun them, and then launch the three pronged advance into the Aitape area. Adachi never slowed his westward movement in forces and supplies, not for an hour; nor did the barges carrying equipment and guns along New Guinea's coast slow their pace.

5th Air Force reconnaissance planes had detected the hordes of enemy troops now moving toward Aitape, and General Kenney ordered a series of air strikes along the entire route between Wewak and Aitape. Col. Dick Ellis of the 3rd Bomb Group took off from Hollandia with all squadrons to bomb and strafe the trails with hundreds of parafrag bombs and chattering .50 caliber nose gun fire. Lt. Col. Charles MacDonald had also brought his 475th Group P-38s southeastward to hit the jungle trails with more bombs and strafing fire. In between, the 70 Wing Beauforts out of Tadji, the 312th A-20 Group out of Hollandia, and the B-24 heavy groups out of Moresby also plastered the dense jungles between the Driniumor and Wewak. During a four day period, 5th Air Force planes dropped 2,500 tons of bombs and expended 200,000 rounds of .50 caliber ammunition.

Further, from offshore, several of Adm. Dan Barbey's destroyers lobbed countless 5″ and 3″ shells into the coastal jungles for several days to stop the Japanese westward movement. The naval shells chopped huge holes in the dank jungle floor, felled trees, and chased lorie and mynah birds, screaming and flapping, into the Toricelli Mountains to the south.

The continuous barrage by American air and naval units had not halted Adachi's persevering troops. While the extensive U.S. assaults took some lives and destroyed some equipment and supplies, the Japanese had reacted deftly to the aerial and sea bombardments. At the first sound of planes or naval guns, 18th Army officers and non-coms directed troops and pack animals off the trails into the deep jungles until the raids had ended. The Japanese also, changed their tactics, moving swiftly during night time hours and resting deep in the thick tropical forests during the day.

The Japanese barges followed the same tactics. The boats hugged the coast and puttered swiftly with loaded supplies during the night, while they hid totally under the overhang of thick branches during the day. Thus the gnarled jungles trees had become a Japanese ally.

As the first week of July passed, reports still funneled into Persecution Force headquarters at Aitape: the Japanese were still on the move. The air and sea attacks had merely delayed the 18th Army, but had not stopped them.

Gen. Charles Hall and Gen. William Gill made frequent treks over the jungle trails from the Nigia River to study the inner defenses at the X-ray and Koronal Rivers, and they had even visited the outer perimeters on the Driniumor.

113

They spoke to Col. Robert Fowler of the 128th, Col. Merle Howe of the 127th, and Col. Peter Hooper of the 112th Cavalry. All of them assured the generals that their men were ready. Meanwhile, the U.S. 124th RCT, with over 5,000 men, was on the way. The regiment was expected to reach Aitape in mid July.

In the trench lines along the Driniumor however, the GIs did not share the confidence of these colonels. The dogfaces sat with taut apprehension, peering over the river at the shadowy green jungles on the other side. They had heard the reports of the Japanese westward movements and they did not appreciate a fight against a horde of zealous enemy troops. Sgt. Jerry Endl of the 128th Regiment's C Company, 1st Battalion, ambled cautiously up and down the trenches of his platoon. Endl had fought the Japanese in both Buna and Saidor and he had learned to respect the fanatic enemy. He carefully checked his two machine gun nests, the mortar teams, the two BAR squads, and the riflemen.

"Everything okay?" He asked the same question of all of them.

The soldiers of his platoon answered Endl with sober silence or with a variety of counter questions. Some stared glumly and said nothing, while others only scowled. A few bombarded the platoon non-com with anxious inquiries: "Sarge, can we hold them?" "Sarge, what'll they do if they capture us?" "Sarge, have we got enough reserves?"

To each question, Endl could only tell them to remain calm, and to avoid panic. The enemy needed to cross 100 yards of open water and the GIs could cut them to ribbons before they got to the west bank. Also, the supporting mortars and light artillery would chop apart more of any charging enemy troops. Still, Endl himself was not sure. He had heard the number: 20,000, and he knew the fanaticism of the enemy. He wondered if these GIs could really stop so many of them. But he continued to check his men, encouraging them.

In the lines of the 127th's 2nd Battalion, in E Company, Sgt. Charles Butler and Sgt. Johnny Watson moved up and down the trenches of the 1st and 2nd Platoons. The E Company non-coms had experienced Banzai charges at Buna and Finchhaven. They remembered the horror of hundreds of hell-bent soldiers storming into withering machine gun fire and artillery explosions with a complete disregard for their lives. Both E Company non-coms knew that men who fought with absolutely no fear of dying could badly rattle any defenders.

Sgt. Butler stopped at a machine gun pit and checked a foursome of men. "Is everything okay?"

"I guess we're ready," Col. Bill Ford said.

"Do you have enough drums?"

"Two dozen."

"Are the barrels good and clean?"

"Just like new," Ford answered. Then the corporal gripped the sergeant's arm. "How soon do you think they'll attack, Charlie?''

"I don't know," Butler shook his head.

"Do you think we can hold?''

"We'd better hold," the platoon sergeant said.

"Yeh," Ford answered, licking his lips and checking the trigger of his .50 caliber machine gun.

The foursome in the pit watched Butler check on other GIs in the platoon. Then, Cpl. Ford studied the murky, narrow river that flowed serenely and slowly northward toward the sea. Next, he squinted into the quiet jungle trees, thick and verdant, on the other side of the river. He listened to the chirps and squeals of lorie and mynah birds deep in the tropical rain forests, the only sounds in the gloomy, dormant brakes across the stream. Ford heaved a sigh and counted his ammo drums again, the tenth time in the past hour.

Further south, on the 128th Infantry's G Company sector, Capt. Tally Fulmer checked his company defenses with his executive officer. His GIs were fully dug in: the riflemen, machine gunners, BAR units, and mortar teams.

"Everything seems in order," the captain told Lt. Bill Howard.

"The men have been strengthening defenses for a couple of days," the executive officer answered the company commander.

"Good." As the duo walked on, the captain stopped and spoke to a platoon non-com, Henry Cooper, who had just checked a machine gun pit. "Sergeant, are the men all right?"

"They're tense, sir," Cooper answered. "A lot of them have been through Nip attacks before and they can't forget that kind of experience."

Fulmer pursed his lips. "It's a trauma, I know. But that's why we're here. Do what you can to keep them loose, sergeant."

"Yes, sir," Cooper answered.

Then the G Company non-com watched his commander and Lieutenant Howard move down the line to visit other GIs in the infantry company lines. Cooper soon turned away, peered into the gnarled trees across the river, and listened to squeals and chirps of tropical birds again. The sound of birds eased Cooper's anxiety; as long as birds chirped in the trees, the Japanese were still some distance away. Cooper wiped the perspiration from his face and walked up the line to keep his men loose, as Captain Fulmer had suggested. However, despite the platoon non-com's encouragement, the GIs could not erase from their minds the dread of a banzai attack.

Further south, in the 3rd Battalion of the Red Arrow Division's 127th Infantry Regiment, the men of I and K Companies sat tensely in the center of the Driniumor River line. In his tent headquarters under a clump of dense trees, Lt. Col. Ed Bloch spoke with Capt. Leonard Lowry and Sgt. Ed. Madcliff. The two companies under the command of Lowry were known as the Lowry Force.

"Captain," Bloch said, "are we in good shape?"

"Yes, sir."

"No gaps in the lines anywhere?"

"None, sir," Captain Lowry said.

Lt. Col. Ed Bloch nodded and then turned to Ed Madcliff. "Sergeant, I suspect those Japanese may be close to the river by now, so we could sure use some up to the minute information. Are you willing to take out another recon patrol for a look?"

"My squad is entrenched in a patch of ground on the river, sir, but if that's what you want, we'll go out again."

"You're the best, sergeant," Bloch said. "We all know that. However, I won't order you out at this late date. It'll have to be on a volunteer basis for you and your men."

"I'll go, sir," Madcliff said, "and I'm sure my squad will go."

"Good," Ed Bloch nodded.

For two days, Ed Madcliff and his squad probed the area east of the Driniumor and they finally spotted a mass of enemy troops on the opposite bank of Niumen Creek, seven miles from the Driniumor River. The Japanese had with them a herd of pack horses which carried dismantled mortars and artillery, along with supplies of shells and ammunition. Further, a number of sentinels guarded the area this time and Madcliff dared not get too near the enemy contingent of troops. Nonetheless, Madcliff could see that the complement of Japanese

118

forces probably numbered 300 or 400 men, perhaps two companies. The sergeant could rightly report that enemy troops were now approaching the Driniumor in force. When he returned to 3rd Battalion headquarters he went immediately to the command post.

"They're coming on strong, sir," Madcliff told Lt. Colonel Bloch. "I guess all those air strikes and warship bombardments didn't do too much."

"Goddamn it," Bloch scowled. He looked at Len Lowry. "Make sure the men are ready. If those Nips are now on Niumen Creek, they could hit us in a day or two."

"We'll be ready," Lowry promised.

Bloch nodded and looked at Madcliff. "I appreciate your efforts, sergeant, even if your reports are hardly encouraging. In view of this dangerous patrol, you and your squad can stay to the rear if you prefer."

"I'd just as soon go back on the line, sir," Madcliff said.

"Sure," the battalion commander grinned.

For three more days the GIs of the 32nd Division's 128th and 127th Regiments remained tense, but alert, in their Driniumor defenses. South of the Red Arrow infantry troops, the GIs of the 112th Cavalry Regiment waited with the same tenseness in their own positions.

At dusk, July 10, as the men on the Driniumor leisurely ate their evening meal of hot bully beef patties and dehydrated potatoes, Sgt. Henry Cooper stopped chewing a mouthful of food.

He had sensed an abrupt strangeness in the surrounding jungle landscape. For a full minute, the G Company platoon leader sat rigidly and curiously. Then he shuddered fearfully. The mynah and lorie birds had stopped chirping and squealing. The Japanese had apparently reached the Driniumor River. Cooper could not see them nor could he hear them, but the sergeant knew the enemy was there. He gobbled the rest of his evening meal, for he needed to remind his men that a Japanese attack might come at any moment.

Cooper's suspicions were well founded. Across the river, less than a quarter mile from the east bank, Col. Mitsujiro Matsumoto of the 78th Japanese Regiment had mustered two companies of men and readied them for a charge across the river. Matsumoto also checked his mortar team who would support this infantry assault. The 78th Regiment, after weeks of preparation and a harsh march through the jungles from Wewak, would make the first attack against Aitape. Matsumoto planned his charge against the American defenses at about midnight, the witching hour for somebody.

Chapter Seven

In the history of military warfare, the 18th Army march from Wewak to the banks of the Driniumor River, especially against continual air and warship attacks, must rank with Hannibal's march through the Pyrenees and Alps. The successful trek from Wewak could be attributed only to the stubborn determination of General Adachi and the troops under him. Although to a lesser degree, the Americans too had endured an agonizing exercise. The GIs had struggled through 25 miles of hostile jungle terrain to reach the west banks of the Driniumor, where they then worked furiously in the insect ridden tropical forests to set up defenses, including a barbed wire wall along the shoreline.

The combatants could not have selected a worse battleground than the New Guinea jungles to conduct a campaign. The terrain represented a land that civilization had forgotten. The rainfall in most areas is often more than 300 inches a year, and on some occasions as much as ten inches fall in a single day. The soldier, sapped of strength while he carried his gear, thus suffered from an incessant rain that often left him constantly drenched.

The jungle itself was a military nightmare. Dense malarial swamps and thick matted brush tested the strength of men with every footstep. Reeking, foul pools of stagnant water exuded a noxious odor of mildewing vegetation, distorted green muck, and gnarled undergrowth. The occasional patches of clearing that interspersed the dense, almost impassable jungles, were usually covered with razor sharp kunai grass, whose blades would cut through a man's clothing and lacerate the skin.

The heat and humidity here were unbearable, soaking the skin with perspiration until a soldier's uniform hung on him like sewage soaked rags, and leaving a pungent, nauseating smell.

In the Aitape area, swift creeks and turbulent streams roared down from the saw toothed Toricelli ridges to settle into sluggish ponds that nourished the larva of malarial mosquitos and other insects. Ugly swarms of bugs continually darted about a man's perspiring face to abet the discomfort of terrain and climate. And there were leeches, armies of them, that clung and tore at a man's legs, arms, and even his face.

In this horrifying arena, the two adversaries prepared for battle. As evening settled over the tropical woodlands on July 10, 1944, the eerie forests darkened into twisted, gnarled silhouettes that resembled distorted phantoms rising from the soggy earth, like alien creatures in a nightmare. Crawling nighttime bugs and buzzing insects harassed the GIs while high humidity left uncomfortable perspriation soaking their bodies under the olive drab fatigue uniforms.

The U.S. infantrymen peered hard at the shadowy trees across the river, expecting a flood of enemy troops to emerge at any moment from the dense brakes.

Sgt. Henry Cooper of the U.S. 128th Infantry's G Company had been uneasy since the sound of birds had ceased at dusk. Bt the time he finished his meal, a nausea foamed in his stomach. The sergeant had accustomed himself to the fare of bully beef, dehydrated spuds, and K rations, but he had never acclimated himself to Japanese banzai charges. Not the food in his stomach, but the thought of a reckless enemy assault had brought the discomfort to his gut.

Cooper shuttled through the darkness to check the men of his platoon. "Keep your belts ready," he told the machine gunners. "Make sure you've got plenty of drums," he told the BAR men. "Be sure you've got enough shells," he told the 60mm mortar crews. "Fix bayonets on those barrels," he told the riflemen. And to all of his platoon GI's, the sergeant reminded them to keep an ample supply of grenades.

"If those bastards reach the barbed wire, the only way you're going to stop them is with grenades."

The men responded positively to Cooper's suggestions. They knew their platoon sergeant had led men successfully in similar jungle fights—at Buna and at Saidor. His instructions had saved their lives in previous fierce battles because the platoon sergeant possessed that sixth sense that had been so vital in the agonizing New Guinea war. So when he issued instructions, the GI's listened.

Cooper had completed a second tour of his platoon when the company commander, Capt. Tally Fulmer, and the executive officer, Lt. Bill Howard, came up to him. "Everything all right, sergeant?" the captain asked.

"Yes sir."

"Remember the orders," Fulmer said. "We don't retreat from the line unless we get permission. The order comes from General Hall himself."

"Yes sir," Cooper said again. But, he felt an inward anger. Hall was safe in his comfortable headquarters back at Aitape, 25 miles to the rear. The general could easily tell men on the line to hold against enemy hordes swarming across the river. Cooper doubted that Hall himself would abide by such a no retreat order if he were overwhelmed by a sea of enemy troops. However, the platoon sergeant did not share his thoughts with Captain Fulmer.

"Are there any weaknesses in the barb wire?" Fulmer asked.

"It's good and sturdy, captain."

The G Company commander nodded. "We've got four 37mm guns for support, one for each platoon. These cannoneers will do what they can, when or if the enemy troops try to cross the river. Of course," Fulmer gestured, "we can't be sure they'll attack our sector. They might strike out at one of the other companies in any of the three regiments strung out from the coast to the mountain foothills."

"Yes sir."

"How about communications?" Lieutenant Howard now spoke.

"We're all set," Cooper said. "We've got two field telephones and four walkie talkies. We'll have adequate contact facilities."

"Good," Howard said.

"One more thing," Fulmer pointed, "be sure your men have enough grenades. If the enemy reaches the wire, grenades may be the only thing to stop them."

"I've already told them that, sir."

"Fine, fine," the captain nodded. Then, he and Lieutenant Howard moved off to talk with other platoon non-coms.

Henry Cooper took one last tour of his platoon trench line, making a final check, before he dropped into his own trench. Three men were waiting there with a .50 caliber machine gun and the GIs looked hard at the platoon leader.

"What does the captain think, sarge?" one of the men asked.

Cooper shrugged. "He didn't tell me anything I didn't already know, and he didn't make any suggestions that I haven't already followed. Are you guys all right? Do we have enough ammo belts?"

"Plenty, sarge," one GI answered. Then he licked his lips. "When will they attack?"

"Who the hell knows," Cooper said. "Maybe in the next few minutes; maybe not 'til tomorrow. We just sit tight and stay alert."

The GI did not answer.

An attack was coming; no doubt of that. On the opposite side of the Driniumor River, Col. Mitsujiro Matsumoto met with his 1st Battalion commander, Lt. Col. Tori Kawakami, and several company officers.

"Most of the Eighteenth Army is now within striking distance of the enemy," Matsumoto said, "but we have drawn the honor of making the first assault against the Americans. I offer you an added incentive to succeed in this assault, for we have learned from our scouts that the Yankee dogs on the other side of the river are the Jungle Lizards of the Thirty-second Infantry Division. In the past, this American division has caused us untold grief. Now, we shall have an opportunity to repay them in kind."

The 1st Battalion officers did not answer, but they recalled well those past battles with the Jungle Lizards. The 32nd Infantry GIs had pushed them into a corner at Gona in January of 1943, during the battle for Buna, and annihilated the defending detachment of the 18th Army. The same Yankee GIs had shoved 18th Army units off the beaches at Finchhaven, over the Huon Gulf plains, and into the hostile Owen Stanley Mountains. And, in February of 1944, these same Jungle Lizards had mauled the 18th

126

Army at Saidor, forcing Japanese troops across the Mot River, up the Galek Track, and again into the mountainous hinterlands. Only a handful of Saidor's Japanese defenders had reached Madang alive.

The Japanese officers of the 78th Regiment's 1st Battalion thus welcomed the chance to strike back; to administer to the Lizards the same death, agony, and suffering that Japanese troops had endured at the hands of the U.S. 32nd Infantry Division troops.

Matsumoto looked at Kawakami. "Are your men ready to attack?"

"Honorable colonel," the battalion commander answered, "our brave soldiers did not come this far to sit idle. They have charged themselves for battle. They are eager to fight; eager to avenge our past losses. When they learn that their adversaries are the Jungle Lizards, they will show even more tenacity in the effort to destroy them."

"Good," Matsumoto nodded. "How many man will make the assault?"

"About four hundred and fifty," Kawakami answered, "every able combat soldier from all three companies in the First Battalion."

"I have assigned a mortar platoon and a light artillery team to support your attack. They will shell the enemy defenses for ten minutes beginning at 2350 hours. Then, at midnight, you will lead your troops across the river."

"Yes, colonel."

Matsumoto now offered Kawatami and his

company commanders a closer look at a map, brightened by the light of a lamp. "This is the sector you will attack. The enemy's defenses are no worse here than anywhere else, but the river current is quite mild. You will attack in three waves, with one platoon from each company in each of these waves. The attack will be on a one hundred yard front. Do you understand?"

"Yes."

"I leave to you, Tori, the details of deploying your men for the assault."

"Yes, colonel," Kawakami said again.

Then, Matsumoto sighed. "May our heavenly ancestors guide and protect you, Tori. May they favor our brave soldiers with success."

"We pray that the spirits will be with us," the 1st Battalion commander said.

Across the river, Sgt. Henry Cooper looked at his watch, squinting in the darkness: 2200 hours. The GIs of his platoon had been sitting here for more than an hour, simply waiting. The passing time, the eerie silence, and the abhorrent darkness only intensified their apprehensions. The dogfaces had found too much time to think, too much time to imagine themselves overrun by enemy throngs; of suffering bloody death from grenade explosions, machine gun fire, bayonet thrusts, or even severed heads from a swinging Japanese sword. The enemy was excellent with a saber in hand to hand combat.

Under dense trees, in a pitched tent that served as G Company headquarters, Capt. Tally Fulmer and Lt. Bill Howard pored over a map on a portable table with the light of a Coleman oil lamp. They studied the company sector, making certain they had prepared all units on the line.

"We didn't miss anything, did we, lieutenant?" Fulmer asked.

"No sir," Howard answered. "We've been on the line twice to make a double check off. Everything is in order."

"What about mortar and artillery?"

"In place, captain," Howard said. When Fulmer only pursed his lips, the executive officer continued. "There's nothing more we can do, sir, except to wait and hope for the best if those Nips come into our sector."

Fulmer nodded. "Call battalion; tell them we're ready."

"Yes sir."

The night brightened as the evening wore on for a shining moon intensified to temper the jungle darkness. The moonlight left a mild illumination on the dense trees across the river and sparkling ripples on the Driniumor itself. The GIs would see the enemy clearly if and when they came out of the brakes. In the trench line and foxholes, the weary Lizards were sleepy, but no U.S. soldier dared to doze off. During the passing hours, since evening mess, the Americans had become more and more convinced that a banzai charge would come during the depths of this July 10-11 night.

Their fears were justified.

At 2350 hours, a sudden staccato of cannon

and mortar fire shuddered the silent jungle along the Drinimor River. Seconds later, bursting orange flashes erupted balls of brilliant light in the dark trees east of the river. The blasts had come from the 51mm mortar tubes and 37mm cannon barrels on the east side of the Driniumor. GIs jerked, confused for a fleeting moment, and then they were aware that the enemy had opened with shelling. The G Company troops cowered deep into their trenches and foxholes, their mouths open to absorb the numbing echo of the cannonade.

As the enemy shells slammed into the patch of jungle, the explosions knocked down heavy limbs, scattered leaves, strewed brush about the area, and dug holes in the jungle floor. The GIs stiffened, but never stirred from their tense, fearful crouches. Many of them pushed their steel helmets tighter on their heads as clods of earth, twigs, and debris rained down on them. Only for a few seconds did some of the Americans peer cautiously over the tops of their holes to view the river where a stillness yet prevailed.

"Stay loose, stay loose!" Sgt. Henry Cooper cried above the din of shells.

But the men only tensed more. Thus far, the mortar and artillery had been quite inaccurate, with most of shells falling behind them. In their shelters, a few men caught dropping fragments of shrapnel to lacerate an arm or neck or leg. No GI had yet suffered death or serious injury. They feared the Japanese would begin a rolling barrage to blanket every square yard of their defense position—from the river bank itself to a depth of perhaps 50 or 60 yards behind these trenches.

However, before enemy shells had squarely hit any of the G Company trenches or foxholes, a sudden rattle of b-blooms erupted behind the Jungle Lizards. American 37mm artillery and 60mm mortar shells answered the challenge from the dark jungles to the east. Soon the GIs saw the bursts of orange balls erupt in acute flashes of light in the brakes across the Driniumor. The heavy U.S. explosions similarly felled branches, while trees crashed downward in some areas. The American cannoneers, who did not know the exact location of the Japanese, tried to blanket a huge area east of the river in the hope of killing the enemy.

The barrage and counter barrage continued for several minutes, with neither side apparently damaging the other very much. The shelling then abated until mere sporadic blasts broke the silence. A quiet returned to the jungle shorelines of the Driniumor. However, the quiet prevailed for only a minute before the G Company soldiers saw darting shapes flitting amidst the trees on the opposite banks of the river.

A moment later, another clamor shattered the silence: ugly numbing cries:

"Banzai! Banzai!"

The chorus echoed along a full hundred yards of treeline that lay squarely away from the G Company perimeter. And again: "Banzai!

131

Banzai'' The renewed cries from across the river sent more chilling fear through the U.S. infantrymen.

Before the G Company Lizards heard the deafening yells die down, a mass of shadows emerged from the trees like a huge coven of black phantoms. The shadows quickly splashed into the river, erupting countless gushers of water along the entire shoreline.

"Banzai! Banzai!"

The Japanese soldiers waded hurriedly through the stream with rifles and machine guns held aloft. As the first wave came a third of the way across the river, American platoon sergeants yelled excitedly. "Fire! Open fire!"

A variety of reverberating volleys spewed into the river: chattering machine guns, burping BARs, cracking rifles, and thumping mortars. Dense blue smoke soon hovered over the water, while orange flashes burst amidst the advancing gray forms. Bullets whizzed in every direction and shrapnel scattered over the stream. The gray shadows fell in clumps, like bowling pins after solid hits. Japanese troops collapsed from rifle slugs in the face or chest or stomach, from multiple machine gun shots that tore off heads and ripped open torsos, or from hot mortar and artillery shrapnel that riddled their bodies.

None of the soldiers in the first wave, 150 men, had even come halfway across the stream before many of them lost their determination and fanaticism. Dozens had died, dozens more had been wounded, and other staggered back in retreat.

The GIs ogled at the schools of dead that now floated and tumbled atop or under the shallow, slow moving Driniumor on its way to the sea. The river had turned red with blood, but from their foxholes, and trenches on the west bank, the Americans could not see the changing color of the water in the darkness. Before the Americans took a grateful breath, however the yells came again.

"Banzai! Banzai!"

Once more a swarm of gray clad troops burst out of the trees and plunged into the river before sloshing through the water. But again, the 78th Infantry troops met a wall of thumping mortar bursts, chattering machine guns, burping BARs, and snapping rifles. And again, the Japanese caught an array of hits that tore many of them to pieces. The dead once more plopped into the water and the wounded once more staggered off in agony. The able, more determined than those in the first wave, continued on, passing midstream and opening fire themselves with rifle and machine gun fire. Some of them hurled grenades, but they were still too far away to reach the G Company Lizards.

The ranks of the pressing Japanese troops rapidly dwindled as the last wave of Lt. Colonel Kakawami's battalion splashed into the stream to fill the vacuum left by dead and wounded. The battalion commander himself had joined this final group to urge his men on in the face of heavy American fire.

"We can overrun them! We can defeat them!" Kakawami shouted to his men.

These last files of Japanese, sloshing past the heaps of bloody, drifting dead in the stream waded recklessly toward the opposite bank. Some of them even scrambled up the shoreline to reach the tangled barricades of barbed wire. As the Nippon soldiers tried to cut their way through, however, dozens of American grenades exploded in their midst, and chunks of shrapnel ripped through their gray uniforms to shatter the flesh and spew blood from their riddled bodies. Not a single 78th Regiment soldier breached the barbed wire before he died.

In the middle of the river, while gesturing frantically to urge on his men, Lt. Colonel Kawakami suddenly caught two .50 caliber machine gun hits in the face. The big slugs shattered his jaw and temple, turning his countenance into a bloody distortion of pulp. The battalion commander threw his hands to his face and then spun around before he toppled into the water. Within seconds he had joined other Japanese dead that rolled and tousled in the shallow stream.

None of the Japanese soldiers in this final wave had reached the American soldiers and survivors of this last group also retreated into the depths of the forest to the east. Then GIs stared at the hordes of gray shapes that now clogged the river, grim evidence that the Americans had ripped apart this first Japanese assault.

In other American perimeters, in the trenches of more 32nd Division units, the Lizards of E Company, I Company, and K Company crouched stiffly in their holes. They had heard the banzai yells and the heavy firing from the G Company sector. However, they could not see what had happened, and their conjectures heightened when a silence returned to the jungle night after the harrowing ten minutes. Some imagined a nightmarish scene of dead fellow GIs, with the Japanese hordes now swarming over slain 32nd Division soldiers to occupy a destroyed G Company area. None of the GIs had dared to leave his own defense position because the Japanese might burst out of the trees and cross the river toward his own trench or foxhole. The GIs, apprehensive and nervous, badgered officers and non-coms for answers. But these superiors had no more knowledge than did the dogfaces themselves.

Some of the radio men in these Red Arrow units called CPs to learn something, but no one in these company headquarters knew anything, either. The lack of information only worsened their fears. Unfortunately the GIs did not know that their fellow soldiers in G Company had hurled back the Japanese banzai charges inflicting heavy losses, leaving countless enemy dead in the Driniumor River.

On the east bank of the river, Colonel Matsumoto listened in horror to the reports of the unsuccessful attack against the American defenders. Out of 450 soldiers in 1st Battalion, only a fraction had escaped unscathed—a mere 30 men. The utter disaster had left the 78th Infantry commander badly disheartened. He had led hundreds of troops on a gruelling, exhausting trek for 80 miles. Had he marched all this distance only to have his men slaughtered on the banks or in the waters of the Driniumor River? Matsumoto cursed the Jungle Lizards of the 32nd U.S. Infantry Division. They had once again mangled a unit from the Japanese 18th Army.

The 78th Regiment colonel than felt an added pang. He needed to call General Miyake to report this complete failure. Matsumoto feared that the Aitape Assault Force commander would react with rage and blame Matsumoto personally for the catastrophe on this first assault.

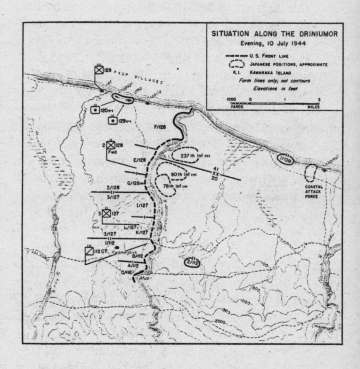

Map shows Japanese assaults with three regiments against American defenses on the Driniumor River during night of July 10-11, 1944

Chapter Eight

Sgt. Charles Butler of E Company's 1st Platoon had been among those who had heard the shooting somewhere to the right in the thick jungles that appeared even more dire in the depths of the night. Now that the shooting and cannonades had stopped, he rose from his foxhole and looked down at the frightened privates in the trenches. They too had heard the banzai yells that had echoed through the night, and they had heard the rattling machine gun fire, the thump of light mortar shells, and the concussions from small artillery. And now, in the dead quiet, the silent landscape seemed more foreboding than the sounds of battle.

The GIs in their muddy trenches and foxholes only licked their dry lips and sipped water from canteens to alleviate their parched throats; or they wiped away heavy perspiration that dampened their faces and necks. The battle some 1,000 yards off to the right was obviously over, but the E Company soldiers did not know whether the Japanese had overrun the G Company positions or whether their fellow GIs had mauled the enemy and thrown him back.

One of the dogfaces looked up at Charlie Butler. "Sarge," he asked softly, "What do you think happened?"

"I don't know," Butler said.

"But you must have some idea. What do you think?"

"I told you—I don't know," Butler answered sharply.

"The little yellow bastards," a corporal grumbled. "I hope G Company killed every last one of the mother fuckers."

"Just stay alert," Butler gestured to his platoon GIs.

The men in the trenches asked no more questions. They squinted into the darkness and at the slow moving Driniumor where moonlight had erupted countless sparkles on the small wavelets—like thousands of fireflies on the water's surface. The river looked serene and inviting, like a lazy stream meandering past some romantic lover's lane. Beyond the river, on the opposite bank, the dense, matted jungle trees looked like a huge ebon silhouette of some demonic creature. The E Company soldiers held their rifles tight, or they checked the ammo drums of their machine guns, or they readied their stacks of 60mm mortar shells. These GIs expected the Japanese to attack their sector of the Driniumor just as the enemy had struck the G Company positions.

Sgt. Butler squinted into the dark trees about him and then looked again at the crouching men in the long trenches. "Stay alert!" he said again. The men did not answer, and the platoon sergeant moved away, walking cautiously up and down the length of the 1st Platoon perimeter to make certain that the rest of the GIs were ready with rifles, machine guns, and mortars. As Butler made his check, the men bombarded him with questions.

"Sarge, do you think they'll hit us?"

"Jesus, Charlie, will they cross the river in front of us?"

"Goddamn, sarge, can we stop a whole goddamn army of those bastards?"

"Charlie, what happened over in G Company?"

To each question, Sgt. Charles Butler shook his head and gave the same response. "I don't know." Then the sergeant warned them again. "Stay alert. If they come, we've got to be ready."

By the time Butler reached the end of his platoon sector, he met the 2nd Platoon non-com, Sgt. John Watson. "Are you guys nervous?" Butler asked.

"What the hell do you think?" Watson huffed. "They heard all that yelling and shooting up the line. They're scared, Charlie, petrified."

Butler squeezed his face. "Do you think they'll come after us?"

140

"They'll come," Watson nodded. "I heard those Nips are jammed in those trees across river like an army of ants. They'll come."

"How the hell can we stop them?"

"I don't know," Watson said, "just fight like hell and shove 'em back like the guys in G Company did."

Butler's eyes brightened. "G Company threw them back?"

"They wiped out a whole goddamn battalion of the sons 'a bitches," Seargeant Watson said. "If they can do it, so can we."

"Yeh," the 1st Platoon sergeant nodded.

While the two sergeants checked the perimeter at the river's edge, Capt. Herman Botcher, the CO of E Company, met with his officers in the company CP tent, about 200 yards from the river bank and deep in the depths of the jungle. "If Fulmer's company threw back that first enemy attack, we ought to be able to do the same thing, if they try to hit our sector."

"Do you think they'll attack us next?" Lt. George Wing asked.

"Your guess is as good as mine," Botcher answered. He then turned to Lt. Bob McClure. "Have you filled that gap on our right flank?"

'Yes sir," McClure answered.

Captain Botcher nodded, spread out a map on the table under a kerosene lamp, and then discussed the E Company defenses with his two subordinates. They would keep at least ten machine guns along the perimeter, a length of

141

1,000 yards—quite thin. Botcher would also keep at least a half dozen mortar teams along the perimeter, spread out about 70 to 80 yards apart. Among the three 37mm artillery pieces assigned to E Company, the captain would keep one piece at each end of the company lines and one piece in the middle of the line. Finally, each rifle team would ahve at least two men with sub machine guns or BARs.

"What about bazookas, sir?" Lieutenant Mc-Clure asked.

"If they attack, they aren't likely to have any armor, so we don't really need anti-tank weapons. However, since we have bazookas available, we can keep at least one bazooka with each rifle team."

Lieutenant McClure nodded.

"Okay," the E Company CO told his two lieutenants, "get out on the line and square away defenses."

"Yes sir," Lieutenant Wing said.

Captain Botcher then called the battalion CP and spoke to Lt. Colonel Henry Geebs, the battalion commander. Botcher asked for more artillery pieces and a full mortar platoon to support his thin line along the river bank. But he got a discouraging answer from Geebs. None were available.

"But we might face an ever bigger assault next time," Botcher protested.

"I can't help it," Geebs said. "We're thin all the way from the coast to the mountains. The best I can tell you is that we'll move reserves into any sector that gets hit.''

"Yes sir,'' Botcher answered with disappointment.

But, Lt. Colonel Geebs himself was not fully confident. His 2nd Battalion was responsible for a two mile length of defense and only three companies were on the line with one in reserve. Luckily, the first Japanese assault at about midnight had been thrown back by Fulmer's G Company, but that was no guarantee they could do so again, and Geebs had no illusions; he expected the Japanese to launch more assaults across the river. The enemy had not prepared themselves for nearly three months to remain immobile on the east side of the Driniumor.

Geebs himself also called for more reinforcements, especially in artillery and mortar units. But the 128th Regiment headquarters gave him the same discouraging answer he had been forced to give Captain Botcher. There were no reinforcements available at the moment.

"We've got every man possible up at the Driniumor line,'' Colonel Fowler said, "and we've got to keep some units in reserve. They tell us that new troops are coming to Aitape in the next two or three days. As soon as they arrive, we'll reinforce all battalions of the 128th. We do have those heavy guns of the One-twenty-ninth Field Artillery and the One-sixty-seventh Tank Battalion, but there's no way to get them through those thick jungles to the Driniumor.

We'll have to settle for the 37mm guns and 60mm mortars. Just hang on, Herm, hang on," Fowler told the 2nd Battalion commander. "I'll do whatever I can as soon as I can."

The American fears of a new assault were justified for the Japanese had no intention of giving up after the disastrous first attack against the G Company positions that had cost the 78th Infantry such heavy losses. General Miyake of the Aitape Assault Force had plenty of troops to send across the Driniumor. Further, the troops were eager because of the coveted booty on the other side of the river: food, clothing, medicine, guns, and most of all atabrine and quinine to stem the heavy casualties from malaria. Many of Miyake's men needed medicine as well as food after the long, tortuous march through 80 miles of jungle from Wewak.

At 0100 hours, an hour after the unsuccessful assault against the American G Company positions, Miyake called into conference his commanders: Matsumoto of the lacerated 78th Infantry, whose 1st Battalion had lost killed or wounded all but 80 of the more than 400 men; Col. Tokutaro Ide of the 80th Infantry Regiment; and Col. Masahuka Nara of the 278th Infantry.

Miyake, Ide, and Nara listened intently as Colonel Matsumoto recapped his unsuccessful assault against the Americans. The enemy was thoroughly dug in, the 78th Regiment commander said. Besides rifle teams, the enemy had an array of automatic rifles, machine guns, mortar, and artillery. The river, more than 200 yards wide, had left the Japanese infantrymen exposed for too long a period as they sloshed to the west bank.

"Colonel," Miyake said, "in view of the unfortunate failure of your First Battalion, do you have any suggestions that may help us to avoid similar losses on a new assault?"

"I believe the next assault should include a much larger number of men," Matsumoto said. "I see no way to breach the enemy defenses except with a large number of troops, in wave after wave. While such a strategy may be quite costly, I believe it is the only way to overwhelm the enemy."

Miyake pursed his lips. "According to our reconnaissance reports, the enemy has defensive positions strung out all the way from the coast line to the foot of the Toricelli Mountains. Our scouts say there are no gaps in these lines, so it appears we have no choice but to make a new frontal assault, this time in force, as Colonel Matsumoto suggests."

General Miyake now told Ide and Nara to prepare three battalions of troops. Colonel Ide would make the first assault with 1,000 men, as opposed to the single battalion the 78th Regiment had used in the first assault. Miyake then ordered Colonel Nara to keep a reinforced battalion, 600 men, directly behind Ide's force to follow the 80th Infantry troops across the river during the height of the assault.

"We must not give the enemy a moment's rest," the Aitape Assault Force commander said. "We must force them to burn out the barrels of their machine guns, rifles, and cannon. Eventually they will collapse. We have thousands of men who made the agonizing march from Wewak under continual enemy air and naval assaults. We cannot fail now, when we have come so close to our objective. As Colonel Matsumoto said, we may lose many men, but the rewards will be worth it."

Colonel Ide and Colonel Nara did not answer, but they knew the rewards of which the general spoke: food for their hungry troops, medicine for their sick, and arms and ammunition to bolster their strength.

General Miyake planned the next assault for 0200 hours on the dark July 11 early morning. He was in the process of planning the assault when Maj. Iwatoro Hoshimo came into the CP tent.

"Please excuse the intrusion, Honorable Miyake, but I come to report that our artillery units have reached this area. A full company of men from the Forty-first Mountain Artillery has moved more than a dozen 75mm cannon close to the west bank. I need only be told where to station them."

Miyake's eyes brightened. "Heavy artillery! Of course! We can heavily bombard the enemy before we attack again." Miyake grinned at the major. "You and your men are to be congratulated for you Herculean accomplishment." The general then referred to a map. "We would like these guns here, for we will make the next assault at this point. Can you move the guns into this position?"

"Yes, general," Hoshimo answered. "I can assure you that the men of the Forty-first will have these guns ready by 0145 hours."

"Very good," Miyake nodded. "We plan our next assault for 0200 hours. That means you can give us a fifteen minute artillery barrage to precede the infantry assault across the river."

"Yes, Honorable Miyake," Hoshimo said.

Miyake then looked at Ide and Nara. "You will prepare your troops for an assault in one hour."

Shortly after the meeting, the regimental commanders alerted their troops and the Japanese infantrymen donned helmets, checked weapons and ammunition, and organized their platoons to strike out in several waves across the Driniumor. Lt. Col. Masanasobu Tsuji mustered his 2nd Battalion with eagerness.

"We will shortly make a new assault against our enemies. Every man must do his duty with courage and determination."

Meanwhile, Major Tadi Yamashita of the 237th's 1st Battalion checked with his officers, Capt. Kuzuo Sugino and Lt. Toshishige Onizuka.

"We will attack behind the troops of the

Eightieth Infantry. General Miyake has determined that only if we use as many men as possible can we defeat the enemy. Also," Yamashita gestured, "we will have heavy artillery support. The capable Major Hoshimo has miraculously managed to bring large cannon to the river bank. The Forty-first Mountain Artillery will begin a fifteen minute barrage at 0145 hours. Then, several waves of troops from the Eightieth Infantry will cross the river at 0200 hours. We will follow them."

The two officers nodded.

"Be sure the companies of our First Battalion are prepared."

The battlion officers then called on non-coms to organize the troops into small squad units. Sgt. Kiyoshi Itoh, a veteran of five years of war, listened carefully to Captain Sugino's instructions before the non-com prepared his men. The troops felt a measure of fear for they knew the fate of the 78th Infantry soldiers that had suffered 90 percent casualties in the first assault. These men of the 237th suspected that they too would suffer heavy losses. But they had two consolations: there would be many more of them, and they would have a heavy pre-attack artillery barrage, as opposed to the futile light mortar support for the 78th Infantry.

An eagerness gripped the 237th Infantry soldiers. They were also aware of the luxuries on the other side of the river. The Americans always had much food, tons of it, and these

Japanese troops knew that the Americans usually abandoned supplied if they needed to retreat hurriedly from untenable positions.

As Sergeant Itoh readied his platoon, one of the men looked hard at the non-com. "Do you believe we can succeed where the unfortunate men of the Seventy-eighth failed?"

"We will succeed this time," Itoh said. "We will have three full battalions in this assault along with the heavy artillery barrage."

"But we have heard that the Americans are heavily armed and well entrenched."

"We will overwhelm them with our sheer numbers," Sergeant Itoh said. "Some of us will die, true, but this is war. And remember, the Americans will leave behind much food and medicine to sustain those of us who survive."

The soldier did not answer, but he knew the non-com was right.

At 0145 hours, the American GIs of E Company were sitting quietly in their trenches and foxholes on the west bank of the Driniumor. They had been staring into the darkness for some time, but they had seen nothing. The GIs had even begun to hope that perhaps the enemy would not make a second assault after the disastrous first assault. But then suddenly, the GIs heard the boom of artillery, loud concussions that apparently came from big guns. Then 75mm shells began exploding in their positions.

The GI's of E Company stiffened and then cowered in their trenches as the shellfire knocked down tree limbs that tumbled to the ground. Other shells unrooted full trees, erupted clods of earth, blew away some of the E Company equipment, or chopped deep holes in the muddy jungle floors. The bower and mynah birds, rudely awakened, emitted frantic screams that challenged the roar of artillery before the birds flew off in squealing terror.

Then came the agonizing screams of dying men as the Japanese 41st Mountain Artillery guns began finding the range. GIs disappeared in thundering bursts, with legs, arms, torsos, and heads flying skyward in the dark jungle night. Some of the holes became nightmarish mixtures of ripped flesh, sticky mud, and flowing blood. Wounded staggered about in horrified dazes, stumbling and falling as they tried to avoid more shrapnel hits. The heavy artillery took a toll against E Company troops compared to the sporadic mortar that had struck the G Company positions earlier.

For 15 minutes the barrage of shells continued unabated. Then, as suddenly as the cannonade had begun, the firing ended. Once more a silence reigned along the banks of the Driniumor, save for the moans of wounded, the occasional screams of the dying, or the dreaded cry of "Medic!"

Sgt. Charles Butler and his men squinted at the quiet emptiness before them. Then, Butler looked at his watch: 0200 hours. He ran a tongue around his dry lips, looked ahead of them, and then rose to his feet. "Stay alert! Stay alert!" he told his men.

The GIs looked at their platoon sergeant, but they did not speak. They turned again to squint across the river and their eyes widened in terror. Like countless gray ghosts rising out of the dark bowels of Hades, the forms emerged from the trees on the east bank of the river. They held their rifles and automatic weapons high over their heads and the weapons glistened in the moonlight. Then came the eerie, numbing cries that shattered the silence.

"Banzai! Banzai!"

Next came a deafening din of fiendish screams, a terrifying crescendo that numbed the eardrums of the E Company GIs. The Americans stiffened again and once more aimed their rifles, automatics, BARs, and .50 caliber machine guns to the east. Soon a myraid of erupting splashes and water geysers dominated the east bank as the gray hordes slogged swiftly into and across the river. Once more they emitted the eerie cries:

"Banzai! Banzai!"

"Open fire! Open fire!"Lt. Bob McClure cried.

The rattle of machine gun bursts, the cracks of rifles, and the thumps of mortar joined the din of shouting Japanese troops. The withering American fire cut down row after row of the gray phantoms, with Japanese dead falling into the river and wounded staggering back to the east bank. Other Nippon soldiers disappeared in eruptions of 60mm mortar and 37mm artillery shells. The river again took on red hue from flowing Japanese blood that had turned the water to an ugly purple.

But still the hordes came on . . . screaming, splashing, and now firing their rifles and automatics. Some of 80th Infantry troops had even swarmed up the west bank before point blank American fire blew away their faces or ripped apart their torses. Yet Japanese troops also scored, killing E Company soldiers with rifle fire and grenades that exploded in trenches and left GI's in twisted, torn, or bleeding heaps.

One group of GIs found themselves in hand to hand combat, warding off and killing Japanese with bayonet thrusts and their own grenades. The Americans held as the enemy finally retreated, leaving countless dead stacked in contorted heaps on the river bank, or drifting atop the surface of the Driniumor like dozens of floating logs.

"We held 'em, sarge, we held!" a GI grinned at Charles Butler.

"Stay alert!" the non-com answered sharply.

Butler was right, for they had barely stopped firing when new waves of Japanese soldiers slogged through the water and past the retreating, macerated ranks of the 80th Infantry's 1st Battalion. Next came Lt. Colonel Tsuji's battalion.

"We must drive on, drive on," Tsuji encouraged his troops.

General MacArthur devised a bold plan to invade Hollandia and Aitape, leap-froging 400 miles and cutting off the Japanese 18th Army.

General George E. Kenny, Commander of U.S.5th Air Force was asked to neutralize Japenese airbases beyond the range of his light bombers and fighters.

Planners for Hollandia-Aitape operation: L to R, Gen. Bob Eichelberger, Adm. Dan Barbey, General Charles Hall, Gen. Walter Krueger, Gen. Ed. Martin

Captain Harry Brown of the 9th Fighter Squadron escorted B-24's on the first bombing raid ever against Hollandia.

Lt. Col. Dick Ellis led low level light bomber attack on Hollandia that destoryed an astounding 116 planes on the ground. He then led 3rd Group in support of the GI's during Aitape land battle.

Lt. Col. Charles MacDonald of the 475th Fighter Group escorted 3rd Group raid on Hollandia. The 475th then support GI's in Aitape jungle fight.

Capt. Len Lowry (L) and Col. Merle Howe (R) listen to Sgt Ed Madliff (R). The sergeant, on a scouting patrol, discovered that Japanese intended to make an all out attack on Aitape.

Lt. Col. Henry Geebs (far right) of U.S. 2nd Battalion rests with his men and native carriers on jungle trail after Japanese force forced him to retreat.

Gen. William Gill, CO of the 32nd Infantry Division (C) talks to his 32nd Division troops during harsh jungle battle.

Col. Bob Fowler, CO of Lizard's 128th Infantry Regiment, suffered two bad defeats by Japanese jungle fighters.

Sgt Gerry Endl won the CMH for his efforts to save eight wounded men during the Aitape battle. He was killed during the fight.

Captain George Royce, CO of U.S. C Company, found himself
and his unit caught in a trap as Japanese overran the American
positions on Driniumor River.

Captain William Dale, CO of the 114th Engineers Battalion, directed his bull-dozers to open paths through the jungle to bring up U.S. 205mm guns.

Major William Lewis, CO of the U.S. 129th Field Artillery, successfully brought his big 205mm and 155mm guns deep into jungle to stop the Japanese offense and to throw the Japanese back.

General Korechika Anami, CinC of the Japanese 2nd Area Forces, got orders from Tokyo to maintain a new defense line in western Pacific to stop any further Allied advance into inner Imperial empire.

General Hatazo Adachi, CinC of the Japanese 18th Army, refused to retreat from his trapped Wewak base. Instead, he directed one of the most amazing jungle counterattacks of World War II in the Pacific.

Lt. Col. Masananobu Tsuji, commander of Japanese 2nd Battalion and a verteran of Singapore fighting, led the initial assault against Americans at Aitape.

Captain Goro Furugori, CO of the 8th Flying Regiment, tried to stop American aerial assaults against Hollandia, but he and his flyers failed miserably. Furugori is seated LEFT; airman on right unidentified.

General Sadahiko Miyake led the Japanese Aitape Assault Force that won early victories in the Aitape battles.

Colonel Masahuko Nara, commander of Japanese Coastal Force, drove the Americans out of their Driniumor River defenses and then drove U.S. GI's out of Anamo.

Captain Sadaaki Akamatsu (seated second from right) tried to support the Japanese ground troops with his airmen from 248th Flying Regiment in Wewak. However, his air units were macerated by American fighter pilots.

Major Iwataro Hoshimo (L), commander of the Japanese 41st Mountain Artillery, amazingly brought his big 75mm guns through 80 miles of jungle to support Japanese attack against the Americans.

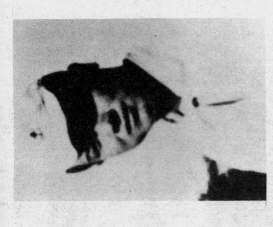

Sgt Kiyoshi Itoh led Japanese retreat with calm efficiency but he was killed in battle.

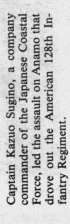

Captain Kazuo Sugino, a company commander of the Japanese Coastal Force, led the assault on Anamo that drove out the American 128th Infantry Regiment.

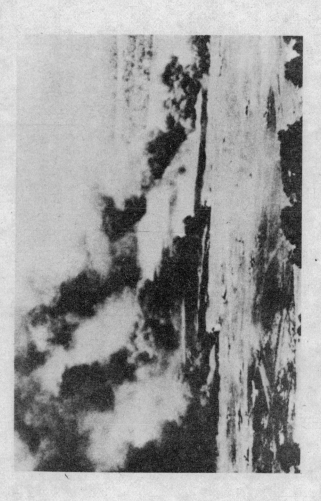

Grounded aircraft at Hollandia burn furiously after U.S. 3rd Bomb Group's devastating low level attack.

A pall of smoke hangs over Hollandia airfields after U.S. 5th Air Force bombers smashed this major Japanese base with heavy air assault.

Rows of destroyed Japanese planes offer grim evidence of 5th Air Force's success in their air attacks on Hollandia.

American GI's hit the beaches at Aitape on 22 April 1944. The surprise leap frog U.S. assault caught the Japanese totally off guard.

GI's unload supplies on Aitape beaches.

The Tadji airdrome at Aitape was the prime objective for U.S. Persecution Force troops. Within 48 hours after Aitape landings, U.S. engineers had repaired field and Australian planes were operating here.

Aerial view of the Driniumor River. Japanese made massive assault against American positions here on the night of July 10-11, 1944, and drove the Americans deep into the jungles.

Battered American GI's, Jungle LIzards of the 32nd U.S. Infantry Division, slog westward through the jungle after heavy assault by Japanese.

GI's continue retreat westward through jungles as Japanese continued their surprising, but massive assaults against Persecution Force troops.

Native carriers bring a wounded Jungle Lizard to the rear on stretcher.

Jungle Lizards of the U.S. 32nd Infantry take a meal break before preparing for new Japanese attacks.

C-47's bring in supplies by air to Aitape to help thwart Japanese advance.

An American GI guards the jungle trail as big U.S. bulldozer plows a swath through the jungle so American troops can bring up big guns to front line.

More big U.S. cannon fire heavy shells into Japanese troops. The Americans' ability to bring this big artillery to the front turned the tide of battle in the Aitape jungle fight.

A big U.S. 155mm cannon, brought deep into the jungle thanks to bulldozers of 114th Engineers opens fire on Japanese positions.

A U.S. Sherman tank growls over improvised jungle road that had been hewed by bulldozer from the U.S. 114th Combat Engineers.

Jungle LIzards of the U.S. 128th Infantry Regiment slosh through jungle stream in pursuit of retreating Japanese.

GI's of 32nd Infantry Division wade across the Driniumor River after driving Japanese headlong to the eastward.

Japanese dead lie in patch of clearing, victims of resurging 32nd Infantry GI's, whose counterattack sent Japanese Aitape Assault Force reeling in retreat.

A Japanese jungle fighter lies dead along the shoreline of the Driniumor River, a stark reflection of Gen. Adachi's defeat in his attempt to recapture Aitape.

Soon the 2nd Battalion Japanese soldiers sloshed through the water and began lobbing grenades into the American positions. Other waves of troops, these from the 237th Infantry, sloshed across the river behind Tsuji's troops. The GIs fired furiously once more, again dropping dozens of enemy soldiers with their heavy fusillade. But the Americans were nearly exhausted and the soldiers of Ide's 80th Infantry and Nara's 237th Infantry pressed resolutely on. Despite the heavy casualties, Lt. Colonel Tsuji, Sergeant Itoh, Captain Sugino, and other leaders urged the men forward.

"Do not falter! Do not falter!" Captain Sugino cried.

The Americans had done a creditable job, but they were only a company of men, with a few light artillery and mortar pieces. They could no longer fend off three battalions of enemy troops. The GIs had already slain perhaps 200 enemy soldiers and sent twice that number staggering in retreat with various wounds. But the heavy fighting had taken a toll. Not only had E Company lost 40 to 50 men of their own killed or wounded, but they were now facing an even worse situation—they were running short of ammunition. The mortar and artillery crews had no more shells, the machine gun teams had no more belts, and the riflemen had few cartridges.

Lieutenant McClure frantically called the E Company CP. "We can't hold them, captain; we can't hold. There's too goddamn many of them, and we're practically out of ammo. We have no more organization and our communications have been broken. If we stay here any longer, they'll wipe us out to the last man."

"Okay, pull back," Captain Botcher said. "H Company has a secondary defense about 500 yards behind our CP. Get everybody you can on the trail. I'll order the other companies on our flanks to dig in."

"Yes sir," McClure answered. The platoon leader quickly passed the word up and down the line. Retreat! The men hurriedly complied as Sergeant Butler, Sergeant Watson, and other non-coms directed the GIs to the rear in an orderly retirement. They left rear guards to pick off the nearest of the advancing hordes.

Meanwhile, Captain Botcher gathered up important papers to join the retreat, while the artillery men spiked their 37mm gun barrels, and mortar men quickly dismantled their weapons.

By 0230 hours, Lt. Col. Tsuji was directing troops through the abandoned American positions, while Sgt. Kiyoshi Itoh was leading squads of men to seize the mounds of food and other supplied left behind by the U.S. E. Company. By 0245 hours, Col. Masahuka Nara himself had crossed the river and soldiers escorted him to the CP, where Major Yamashita was rummaging through everything here.

"Have you found anything worthwhile?" Nara asked.

"Nothing, Honorable colonel," the major

answered. "The Americans, unfortunately, conducted a wise and orderly retreat. They left behind no papers, no maps, nor anything else of any worth."

"But they did leave behind considerable stores of food and medicine," Captain Sugino grinned at the colonel. "For the first time in many weeks, our troops can enjoy a nourishing meal to stem their hunger. They will have atabrine to stop the epidemic of malaria. Besides capturing these precious supplies, colonel, we have also opened a huge hole in the enemy's defenses. Perhaps the Tadji airfields are now within our grasp."

Colonel Nara squinted into the dark cover of dense tree branches overhead and he then looked at Major Yamashita. "While I am grateful for capturing these needed supplies and breaching the enemy's defenses, we cannot become complacent.

"Honorable Nara, perhaps we should build strong bunkers at once for we can expect enemy air attacks in the morning," Major Yamashita said. "We should be well sheltered to avoid serious losses from such assaults."

"But the enemy is on the run, Honorable Nara," Captain Sugino disagreed. "Surely, we should press our attack."

"Perhaps," the 237th Infantry commander nodded. "We will contact Aitape Force headquarters and determine if General Miyake wishes to make more assaults during these dark hours."

"I will find a radio man," Captain Sugino said.

However, before Sugino acted, a radio man himself walked into the CP tent. "Honorable Nara, we have established contact with Aitape Force headquarters."

"Good, good," Nara nodded. "General Miyake will be happy to learn of our successful assault against the enemy to establish the first bridgehead across the Driniumor River. We must also ask him what he wishes us to do next." He then gestured to the radio man. "Please contact General Miyake personally."

"Yes, colonel," the radio man said.

Chapter Nine

The Japanese breakthrough against E Company had opened a strategic hole in the American defenses. As soon as Gen. Sadahiko Miyake learned of the bridgehead from Col. Masahuko Nara, the general immediately ordered other units across the river and into the gap. Further, he ordered more big guns of the 41st Mountain Artillery brought up to the river bank to support further action against the Americans. He also ordered a mass of service troops to carry supplies across the river behind the combat jungle fighters. Then, the Aitape Assault Force commander called his regimental colonels and Major Iwataro Hoshino into a quick conference.

"We must take advantage of our good fortune. I have ordered support troops and provisions across the river to consolidate our positions, while we continue our attacks." He looked at Colonel Nara. "How big is the breach?"

"About two hundred yards wide and perhaps several hundred yards deep."

"We cannot give the enemy any rest," Miyake gestured. "We will launch a new attack no later than 0300 hours. I want the other two battalions of the Seventy-eighth Regiment to prepare for an assault across the river to make an attack to the south. I would also ask that Colonel Nara's Coastal Force mount an assault on the north of this breach." He looked at Major Hoshimo. "Is it possible that some of the big artillery can be moved to both south and north to aid in these attacks?"

The major grinned. "I anticipated such a request, Honorable Miyake. I was not content to merely move these guns forward. Artillery pieces are already moving to our right and to our left."

The general returned the grin. "It is no wonder that the Honorable Adachi has great faith in you, major."

Hoshimo placed a finger on the rough map atop the crude table. "We are also dismantling some of the 75mm guns and putting them on pack animals to cross the river here, in the area of the breach. We hope to have at least six such guns across the river within an hour." He looked at Colonel Ide. "I thought you might want these weapons to support further advances west of the river," he told the 80th Regiment commander.

Ide grinned. "You have anticipated my wishes, also, Major."

"We will have these guns reassembled on the other side of the river in time for new assaults at 0300 hours," Hoshimo said.

"Good," Miyake nodded.

"Meanwhile, ten 75mm guns are now moving to the northern sector and ten 75mm guns are moving to the southern sector. The remainder of our battalion's big guns are still coming up the trails from Wewak. When they arrive, we will assemble them and deploy them wherever you feel it is necessary. Our major problem is that we have only a limited supply of shells for these cannon."

"Then you must make every shell count," Miyake said. "Let us hope that barges will soon bring us more shells as well as other supplies we need quite badly." Then the Aitape Assault Force commander turned to Colonel Nara. "Can the units of the Two-thirty-seventh Regiment make an attack in the north by 0300 hours?"

"We have two battalions of jungle fighters already in position to cross the river," Nara said. "We also have 37mm cannon and 51mm mortar guns in place to aid us. We will attack as soon as you give the order, general."

"And you, Mitsujiro?" Miyake asked the 78th Regiment commander.

"We are ready to cross the river to the south," Colonel Matsumoto answered.

Miyake nodded and then looked at Colonel Ide. "You have done well, Tokutaro, but you cannot rest, even though your troops have just completed an agonizing assault across the river. You must leave to supply troops the duties of amassing the captured enemy supplies and any weapons that are still useful. As soon as the big guns from Major Hoshimo's battalion are across the river, you will continue to push inland. You must divide your units and expand your bridgehead by attacking both north and south as well as west."

"Our troops are eager," Ide said. "I will notify the battalion commanders to ready their soldiers for such new assaults."

"Fine," Miyake said. He then squinted at his watch. "The time is now 0130 hours. In an hour and a half, at 0300 hours, we will begin these multiple assaults. I want artillery and mortar barrages to start by 0250 hours. Let us hope we attain our objectives by daylight."

"We will do so," Colonel Ide promised.

Meanwhile, the Americans tried to recover from the reeling enemy assault that had brought the breach in the Driniumor River lines. After the stragglers of E Company reached the sanctuary of the H Company lines, Captain Botcher met with the H Company commander.

"Christ, Herm," the H Company commander said, "they must have hit you with a whole army. G Company threw them back and I can't believe that your boys couldn't have done the same thing."

"They came on like locusts," Botcher said.

"There was no way to contain that horde. We were practically out of ammunition and they were still coming on."

"We'll assign your men to positions in our lines here. They'll be good reinforcements. I think the Nips will try to come further west and we'll need to defend ourselves with as many men as we can."

The H Company commander then sent his executive officer with Captain Botcher and Lieutenant McClure among this unit to find places for the E Company soldiers. The GIs of H Company could only gape at the tattered, tired newcomers. They stared uneasily at these withdrawn troops, whose uniforms were covered with blood or mud, or whose legs, arms, heads or torsos were covered with hasty bandages.

By 0200 hours, the visitors had settled into positions and men like Sergeant Butler, Sergeant Watson, or Corporal Ford recounted the tale of horror along the Driniumor River line. Their fellow soldiers listened with apprehension.

Further back, at the field headquarters of Percussion Force, Col. Bob Fowler of the 32nd's 128th Regiment and Col. Merle Howe of the 32nd's 127th Regiment met with Gen. William Gill, the Red Arrow Division commander. "General Hall is quite upset with the break in our lines. He had asked that we make no withdrawals without orders."

"They couldn't stop a storm, general," Colonel Fowler said. "There were simply too many of them and the E Company troops almost ran out of ammunition. Captain Botcher had to give a retreat order and he was lucky to get most of his soldiers back to the H Company lines. He lost about twenty men killed and twenty more wounded."

"Still," Gill said, "those Nips must be pouring troops by the hundreds into that gap right now."

"The E Company personnel are set with H Company in this secondary defense line and they'll try to hold," Fowler said. "Meanwhile, I've had more artillery and mortar moving into the First Battalion defenses to the north. I've also ordered new defenses on the flanks in case the Japs try to hit us from the breach."

Gill did not answer. He looked at Colonel Howe. "What about your battalion?"

"The Lowry Force is in good shape, sir," the 127th Regiment commander said. "I've asked them to build a defense line facing the breach and I've also called for more artillery and mortar units."

"They've got to hold," Gill said, frowning. "We can't let those Nips expand their bridgehead. We'll have Fifth Air Force make air strikes in the morning. If we keep those Nips in that pocket 'til then, maybe our bombers can destroy them."

The regimental colonels did not answer.

The 32nd Infantry commander now looked at the map on his portable table. "We can't ask for reinforcements from the One-twelfth Cavalry forces," Gill said, "because they've got to protect the southern sector against any Japanese assault across the river. If worse comes to worst, I'll have to decide whether to retreat into the One-twelfth positions or to have Colonel Hooper send reinforcements from the One-twelfth into any new gaps in the line." He sighed and then continued. "I can't ask the troops on the X-ray and Koronal Rivers to come east. They've got to stay put in these secondary defenses. The men you have in the Driniumor area will simply need to do the best they can. If you hold for the night, I'm sure the air force will take care of those Nips come daylight."

"What about those reinforcements? The One-twenty-fourth Regiment?" Colonel Howe asked.

"They're on the way," Gill said, "that's all I know."

"How about the heavy guns from the One-twenty-ninth Field Artillery?" Colonel Fowler asked. "Can we bring them forward?"

"There's no way to get those big 205s or even the 155s over the narrow jungle trails east of the Nigia River."

"But those Nips get their big guns and mortar through the jungle," Fowler said. "That cannon did a horrible job on E Company."

"I know," Gill nodded. "The Nips have shown great ability to dismantle them quickly, carry the parts on horses, and then reassemble them in a hurry. We can't do the same thing with those monsters of ours; they're simply too big. But, we'll use those 205s and 155s if the Japanese breach our secondary defenses on the Koronal and X-ray Rivers. No, I'm afraid you'll need to be satisfied with the 37mm guns and 60mm mortar. But maybe we can bring up some of the heavier 80mm mortar.''

"Yes sir," Fowler said.

"As I said," the 32nd Infantry commander continued, "General Hall is quite upset. He's asked that you make every effort to stop the enemy from here on. Please return to your units; relay the general's feelings to your battalion and company commanders. Make sure your men have plenty of ammunition and make every effort to hold these positions unless it becomes absolutely necessary to withdraw.''

"Okay, general," Colonel Howe said.

When the meeting broke up, about 0130 hours, Howe and Fowler returned to their respective field headquarters and spoke to their commanders. Lt. Col. Henry Geebs of the 128th's 2nd Battalion, after meeting with Fowler, felt little optimism. He had taken the brunt of the Japanese assault so far. While, his G Company had repelled the first attack, his E Company had wilted before the second and more massive attack.

"They've got thousands of troops, Bob," Geebs said. "They can overrun us with sheer numbers. If they attack again tonight in heavy force, I doubt if we can stop them, not without reinforcements and those heavy guns from the One-twenty-ninth Field Artillery.''

"We've got to hold, Henry," Fowler said.

"We were goddamn lucky this time," Geebs shook his head. "Captain Botcher was able to extricate most of his troops in an orderly retreat. The next time those bastards might run right over us.''

"Maybe we won't have any more attacks tonight," Fowler said. "G Company left a lot of supplies behind and that may be a blessing. The Nips may be so ecstatic over this booty, they might not think of anything else tonight except to wallow in their good fortune. Those mounds of food, medicine, and other provisions must have intoxicated them after that trek from Wewak. In the morning, we'll have air strikes.''

"Christ, Bob," Geebs huffed, "the Nips know they'll get hit with air strikes in the morning. They aren't going to sit around celebrating for the rest of the night." He looked at his watch: 0200. "I'd guess they'll hit us again soon, maybe within the next hour.''

"Then goddamn it, Henry, make sure your G and H Company troops are ready," the 128th commander said acidly. "Tell them they've got to hold.''

"Yes sir," Geebs answered with a tinge of formality.

At the 127th Regiment headquarters, Lt. Col. Ed Block of the 3rd Battalion felt no more confident than did Henry Geebs. "Without re-inforcements or those big guns from the 129th Artillery," he told Colonel Howe, "I don't think we can hold back the kind of assault that overran the One-twenty-eighth positions."

"You're strong," the 127th commander answered. "You've got plenty of ammo and plenty of weapons. They'll need to throw a whole division at you to breach the Lowry Force lines."

"And they might do just that," Bloch said.

Howe looked at Capt. Leonard Lowry. "Well?"

"Sure, we're dug in," Lowry answered. "We've got two full companies, plus a mortar platoon and some 37mm artillery pieces. We could hold off a battalion of troops, maybe even two battalions. But I'd guess the Japanese succeeded in their second charge because they used an entire regiment in the banzai charge. If they throw a couple thousand troops at us, I don't think we can stop them."

"Look," Howe gestured, "at the moment, we can't get those big guns, and we can't get rein-forcements. We won't have air help until morning. I'll try to get General Hall to use some of the One-twelfth Cavalry troopers to help out. And, if General Hall won't release them and you can't stop an attack, you'll have to fall back into the One-twelfth positions."

"Yes sir," Captain Lowry said.

While the Americans once more dug in on this

dark night, the Japanese poised themselves for the upcoming multiple assaults. At 0250 hours, Major Hoshimo's 75mm artillery and 90mm mortar units opened with a barrage from the east bank on the north and from the east bank on the south. Other big guns opened from the newly won ground west of the Driniumor. Cannon and mortar shells pummeled the 128th Regiment positions in the north, while other shells struck the Lowry Force position in the south and the combined E and H Companies to the west.

Once more the GIs of the 32nd Infantry Division cowered in their foxholes and trenches, blinking and grimacing as orange balls erupted in their midst and sent shrapnel in all directions. The Japanese cannon now appeared more accurate, for some of the 75mm and 90mm explosions tore up foxholes about the Lowry Force positions to the south, the 128th positions to the north, and Lt. Colonel Geebs' G and H Company positions to the west. Numbing blasts blew away legs, arms, heads, and torsos. Blood flowed heavily from the pulverized bodies of dogfaces and left sticky, sanguine pools in foxhole mud. For ten minutes the barrage continued and then, as before, the guns abruptly went silent.

Weary GIs on the line understood the meaning of the sudden quiet. The Japs were about to attack. In his shelter, Sgt. Ed Madcliff looked at his watch: 0300. Madcliff then peered over the edge of his foxhole to see the gray hordes splashing into the river, screaming in deafening yells as they sloshed westward.

"Banzai! Banzai!" The cries hurt Madcliff's eardrums.

The Japanese braved withering machine gun, BAR, and rifle bullets that poured into their ranks. Swarms of the dark shadows fell from the intense fusillade, but still they came on. Madcliff scurried up and down the line to urge his men to stand firm.

"You've got to hold 'em back."

I and K Company dogfaces seemed to be holding their own. And, in fact, Colonel Matsumoto himself had lost some of his confidence as his men fell in droves from the withering American fire. He screamed at his troops and he gestured frantically to encourage his men on.

Then the 78th Regiment commander got help.

Lt. Col. Masanasobu Tsuji had been among the first unit commanders to reform his troops on the west bank of the Driniumor. He had already atoned for his mistake on the Harech River by leading his troops into the U.S. E Company positions. Now, his appetite whetted, he had counted the minutes restlessly until the order came to attack. Finally, at 0300 hours, he ordered his battalion forward and his men responded eagerly.

"Banzai! Banzai!"

The GIs of I Company heard the cries from the north and they stiffened when they saw the new mass of gray shapes emerge from the jungles. Tsuji, brandishing a sward, directed his troops southward and the 2nd Battalion soldiers stormed ahead, tossing a cascade of grenades into the American lines. Exploding shrapnel ripped apart many of the Lowry Force foxholes. Tsuji's men also unleashed withering machine gun fire that picked off American soldiers. The dogfaces worked hard, but their limited numbers were not enough to cope with the endless swarms of enemy troops now coming out of the jungle as well as across the river to the east.

Captain Lowry called the 112th CP to the south. "We need help. Send us up some help."

"We can't do that, captain," somebody answered. "We've got orders to stay put right here with every man we've got."

"But they're clobbering us," Lowry cried frantically.

"Then get the hell out of there," the voice answered. "Withdraw your troops south into our lines. We've got a good perimeter around Afua on our flanks as well as on the river itself."

"But we'd be giving up ground," Lowry said. "They'll widen their bridgehead."

"I can't help that, captain. You can bring your men south. That's all I can tell you."

"Okay," Captain Lowry sighed. He then called his platoon leaders. "Withdraw! Withdraw to the south! We'll try to make the One-twelfth Cavalry lines."

"Yes sir," somebody answered.

Moments later, the GIs of Lowry Force pulled

out of their trenches and foxholes and scurried southward. Cool-headed squad and platoon sergeants like Ed Madcliff kept panic to a minimum and led most of the GIs safely through the jungle until they found sanctuary within the 112th Cavalry lines.

Lt. Colonel Tsuji hurried in pursuit with his 2nd Battalion, while Colonel Matsumoto himself breached the river bank with some of his 78th Regiment soldiers to overrun the abandoned American positions.

To the west, deep in the jungle, the weary men of Captain Botcher's combined E and H Company cowered from the heavy mortar and artillery fire that spewed through the jungles and into their ranks. Lt. Col. Henry Geebs zigzagged frantically through the American positions, but the heavy fire was tearing them apart.

"We've got to pull back," Captain Botcher insisted.

"They want us to hold," Geebs said.

But, the mortar-artillery barrage had barely ended when hordes of Nippon troops poured westward out of the jungles. "Banzai! Banzai!" The dark shadows from the 80th Infantry Regiment came in waves, unleashing withering fire and nearly overrunning the two American companies. Geebs finally issued a reluctant order to his GIs:

"Pull back! Pull back! We'll try to make Chinapelli."

Moments later, the GIs scrambled out of their

holes and fled hastily westward through the dark, thick jungles. Geebs, Botcher, McClure, and the others of the 128th's 2nd Battalion would not stop until they reached the safety of Chinapelli on the Nigia River.

In the north, after the same preliminary heavy artillery and mortar barrage, Japanese troops sloshed across the Driniumor to attack the 1st Battalion of the U.S. 128th Regiment. The GIs sent withering machine gun, rifle, and BAR fire into the countless shapes. The fusillades mowed down dozens of Nippon soldiers like scythes cutting through wheat fields. But despite heavy losses, Colonel Nara drove his 237th Regiment troops on. A few of the Japanese came more than halfway across the river before they met death or staggered back with bloody wounds. Fowler believed his 128th Regiment had stopped the enemy.

But then, a murderous barrage of mortar fire, both 51mm and 90mm, arced into the 1st Battalion lines of the American regiment. The barrage chopped up foxholes, killing and wounding dozens of GIs; and the barrage ignited mounds of supplies, felled trees, and sent limbs crashing into American positions. The new attack from the south flank numbed the Americans who now faced a charging horde of Japanese troops from the jungles to the south as well as the Driniumor River.

Colonel Fowler dashed amidst the exploding shells to check his defenses. ''Hang on, hang on!

Keep an eye on the flanks!''

Capt. George Royce of C Company, holding his helmet, zigzagged up to the regimental commander. "The barrage is too heavy, sir. They're chopping us to pieces. We don't have time to dig deep and a lot of our men are catching heavy shrapnel in those improvised shallow holes."

"Hold," Fowler insisted. "I'll try to get counter barrage up here."

But the heavy Japanese shelling had kept the 1st Battalion pinned in their holes, while the hordes of 237th Regiment soldiers under Nara continued to slosh across the river, while Colonel Ide's 80th Regiment troops poured out of the dark forests, rushing headlong toward the American south flank.

"Banzai! Banzai!"

An almost sadistic grin creased the face of Col. Tokutaro Ide. He had plowed through the G Company positions earlier and sent them reeling westward into the jungle. Now he was pouncing on the American C Company of the 128th U.S. Regiment. The Japanese colonel gestured eagerly to his subordinate. "Captain," he cried to Toyozo Kitazono, "take the enemy positions along the river."

"Yes, colonel."

Then, Ide yelled to another subordinate. "Lieutenant, you will force an attack on my left."

"Yes, colonel."

The 1st Battalion of the Japanese 80th then

pushed forward, lobbing grenades, unleashing heavy machine gun fire, and pouring rifle fire into the American positions. The GIs fought back vigorously, even as they endeavored to ward off other 41st Division Nippon troops sloshing across the river. But, the two-pronged assault sapped the strength of the American defenders. Many of the GIs were dead or badly wounded. The defenses had been broken in a dozen places because the Japanese had sent too many soldiers into the charge.

"We can't hold, captain," Sgt. Gerry Endl cried.

"Are you sure, sergeant?"

"If we stay here, they'll flatten us; kill every one of us."

Captain Royce hesitated until he got a call from Colonel Fowler. "We can't hold them, captain. The First Battalion is pulling back to Anamo. The Nips are pouring up the west bank north of you. Get your company the hell out of there and head northwest to Anamo. We've got pretty good defenses there."

"Yes sir," Royce answered. Then he called Gerry Endl. "Sergeant, we're pulling out, back to Anamo. Get the word out and start moving."

"Yes sir," Endl said.

But as the GIs of C Company pulled out of their holes and hurried northwest through the dark jungle thickets, they ran into heavy enemy fire, including grenade and machine gun fire. Some of Colonel Nara's 237th groups had not only breached the river bank north of Royce's U.S. infantry company, but the Japanese had swept nearly a mile inland. C Company was cut off and trapped. 200 men, including their attached mortar platoon, were caught in a pincer.

"Get them back, get them back," Captain Royce cried. "There's a mass of Nips up ahead."

"Yes sir," Sgt. Gerry Endl cried. He then turned and gestured to his GIs. "Hold up! We're going back."

"Back!" somebody yelled. "Jesus Christ, sarge, they're pouring in like ants from the east and south."

"They've got us cut off to the north," Endl said.

The sergeant then joined Captain Royce and other officers and non-coms to quickly muster the men into a patch of jungle where the GIs hastily dug trenches in a wide circle. Fortunately, the swift movement of the Japanese across the river and to the south had left the 18th Army soldiers quite extended and scattered. Colonel Nara needed to hold up his advance northward through the jungle until he reorganized his forces to continue the advance. The 237th Regiment commander would need to spend a couple of hours in this task. By then, C Company would be dug in along with their weapons, including the mortar tubes and machine guns.

Meanwhile, the remainder of the retreating 1st Battalion had joined the 128th's retreating 2nd

Battalion and hurried towards the strong defense positions at Anamo on the coast. Here Colonel Fowler's GIs would be relatively safe. Beyond them was the sea where not Japanese, but U.S. destroyers loitered ominously. The American ships from offshore could bombard enemy units with telling 5" and 3" shells if the Japanese tried to cross the open Kunai grass plains to assail Anamo.

The Americans however, could hardly feel elated or confident. In the south, the Japanese had chased the American Lowry Force into the 112th Cavalry positions. In the center, Lt. Col. Henry Geebs' battered and bloody troops of H and E Company had fled westward all the way to Chinapelli, a village halfway between the Driniumor and Nigia Rivers. In the north, the 128th units under Col. Robert Fowler had retreated all the way to Anamo on the coast. And worst of all, 200 men of C Company under Capt. George Royce were entrapped in the jungles southeast of Anamo with little prospect for relief.

The Japanese assaults on the night of July 10-11 had elated General Adachi. His troops had opened a huge gap nearly three miles long and 1300 yards deep beyond the Driniumor. "You have done well, Sadahiko," the 18th Army commander congratulated his Aitape Assault Force commander. "The enemy is now reeling and confused. May I suggest that you dig in your troops quite thoroughly. You must rest during the daylight hours. Perhaps we can resume the drive to the Tadji airdromes sometime tomorrow night.''

"The troops are tired, but their morale has never been higher," Miyake said. "We have won much food, medicine, blankets, clothing and atabrine. Our men will get a good meal and our sick will get treatment. We will regain our strength for new assaults on our enemy.''

"Excellent," Adachi said. "Please accept my gratitude to both yourself and the men of your command.''

"Thank you, Honorable Adachi.''

By 0530 hours, hundreds of Japanese troops had occupied the huge pocket west of the Driniumor River. They had dug chasmic trenches and covered them with thick logs. Then, as the first hint of dawn emerged from the east, the Japanese troops disappeared into their holes as vampires vanished into their coffins at the same stroke of dawn. As the brightness of daylight was a fatal enemy to vampires, so too were the U.S. 5th Air Force bombers in daylight a fatal enemy to the Japanese soldiers.

Chapter Ten

When Gen. Korechika Anami heard of the Japanese success on the banks of the Driniumor, he gaped in utter astonishment. He had never believed that Adachi would succeed with his daring plan, a seemingly impossible venture against superior enemy forces. Anami, in fact, felt a begrudging admiration for the 18th Army commander who had fired his troops to march through 80 miles of hostile jungle and then win a battle against a strong, entrenched enemy. The 2nd Area Forces commander sent a congratulatory radio message to Wewak, but Adachi read the communication with disdain and he returned a caustic message of his own.

"Our troops have succeeded even without the full support of the Second Area headquarters. My valiant soldiers accomplished this feat in spite of those who have all but abandoned them. But, Honorable Anami, you can still participate in this sweet victory. The battle for Aitape is not yet won and we need more provisions, fresh troops to relieve my tired soldiers, and more aircraft to support our offensive. I would rather have a barge of supplies than a thousand letters of congratulations. I will myself leave for the front to take personal command of this operation. We expect this campaign to end in the capture of the Tadji airdromes, a glorious victory for the jungle fighters of the Eighteenth Army."

After a dawn breakfast on July 11, Adachi left Wewak to march over the long weary jungle trail to join General Miyake on the Driniumor River.

To the north, the troops of the Aitape Assault Force remained well sheltered in their newly constructed defenses to await expected air attacks on the morning of July 11, and the U.S. 5th Air Force did not disappoint the Japanese. At first light, on Sentani Field and Cyclops Drome respectively in Hollandia, the ignition of A-20 and P-38 engines erupted in heavy whines across the Sentani Plateau that paralleled Lake Sentani, 125 miles north of Aitape. Ground crews had loaded both the Havocs and the Lightnings with frag bombs, hundred pound demo bombs and .50 caliber machine gun belts.

In the U.S. 3rd Bomb Group operations tent, Lt. Col. Dick Ellis briefed his pilots and gunners, referring to a map on a portable slate board behind him. "As far as we can tell, the Japanese had established themselves here," he told his airmen, "on the west bank of the Driniumor River. Persecution command at Aitape believes they've occupied a patch of jungle about fifteen hundred yards deep and two miles long. We've been told that our own troops have withdrawn to Anamo here in the north, to Afua in the south, and to the banks of the X-ray River to the west."

"That's quite a breach, colonel," Maj. Ken Rosebush of the 3rd's 90th Squadron said. "Can we saturate an area that big?"

"The Four-seventy-fifth Fighter Group will also be hitting the area with two squadrons of fighter-bombers," Ellis said. "While we hit the areas in the northern sector, they'll hit the areas to the south."

"Can we expect any enemy air opposition?" Rosebush asked.

"We don't think so," the 3rd Group commander said, "but we'll have one squadron from the Four-seventy-fifth Group to escort us. The Nips do have some planes in Wewak, so we might run into a few Zeros." He paused and then continued. "We'll be using all four squadrons this morning. The Eighth Squadron will go in first, then the Thirteenth, the Eighty-ninth and the Nintieth Squadron in last. Each squadron will cover a two hundred yard band. Any questions?"

None.

"Okay, man your aircraft. Take off is at 0600 hours."

At Cyclops Drome, Lt. Col. Charles Mac-Donald of the 475th Fighter Group also briefed his airmen. "We're going out this morning with

179

the Third to hit the Nips on the Driniumor River," the 475th commander also referred to a map. "This is where the Nips broke across the Driniumor and established a bridgehead. They've taken an area about two miles wide and fifteen hundred yards deep. The Third Group will go in first to hit the northern sector and we'll be right behind them to hit to the south."

"What about opposition?" Maj. Tom McGuire asked.

"That'll be your job," MacDonald pointed. "Your Four-thirty-first Squadron will be our escorts. One and Two Flights will cover the Third's light bombers and Three Flight will cover our P-thirty-eight fighter-bombers."

"Okay," the 431st Squadron major answered.

Tom McGuire had already achieved a phenomenal record in the Southwest Pacific. He had been in the New Guinea war for more than a year and during that time he had scored 30 victories, a record only second to Richard Bong, America's leading air ace. Before McGuire concluded his astonishing career as a fighter pilot, Tom McGuire, from Paterson, N.J., would score 38 victories and earn a Congressional Medal of Honor.

"Are there any questions?" MacDonald asked. When no one answered, he nodded. "Okay, I'll take the Four-thirty-second Squadron in first to cover the two hundred yard sweep, and the Four-thirty-third Squadron will cover the southern stretch. Make every bomb count. If those Nips get themselves organized today, they could push even deeper into our ground positions." He looked at his watch. "Please synchronize: 0540 hours. Take off is at 0605. We'll rendezvous with the Third Group south of Hollandia and hit the target area about 0640 hours, only an hour from now."

By 0550 hours, the airmen of the 3rd Bomb Group and the 475th Fighter Group were climbing into their aircraft and at 0600, a green light blinked from the control tower on Sentani Field. Lt. Col. Dick Ellis revved his A-20 engine and then zoomed down the runway with his wingman. Within moments, 52 more A-20s of the 3rd Group had climbed skyward. At Cyclops Drome, Lt. Col. Charles MacDonald caught the blinking all-go green light at 0605 hours and he too revved the twin engines before he zoomed his Lightning fighter-bomber down the runway with his wingman. Soon, 42 more P-38s of the 475th were also airborne. By 0615 hours, the two U.S. air groups had rendezvoused, turned south, and headed for Aitape.

Above the A-20 light bombers and P-38 fighter-bombers, Maj. Tom McGuire held his P-38s in loose formation, sending two Lightnings far ahead to keep alert for any Japanese interceptors. However, the American air leaders considered this mission on the morning of July 11 as a milk run, with no expected air opposition and little or no anti-aircraft opposition. Their

181

only concern was to hit the enemy troops hard enough to send the Japanese soldiers scurrying back across the Driniumor River.

But the mission would be something more than a milk run. Capt. Sadaaki Akamatsu still had a little sting left. At Boram Field in Wewak, the 248th Flying Regiment commander had also briefed his airmen for a morning strike. "You have heard of the glorious victory last night by the troops of the Eighteenth Army. They have established a strong position east of the Driniumor River, and they will continue their push to the Tadji airdromes. We must do our part in striking our enemies this morning in a strong air attack."

The captain moved his finger on a map. "Our troops are here and the enemy has retreated into new positions to the north, west, and south. I was told that General Miyake plans to continue his drive to capture Chinapelli and Palauru before he makes a final assault across the Nigia River to take the airdromes. We can help in this cause by disrupting these enemy positions."

"Where will we attack?" Lt. Toru Kurosawa asked.

"Here, at Anamo to the north, and here, at Afua to the south," Captain Akamatsu referred to his map. "We must neutralize the enemy forces in both areas so they cannot strike the flanks of our ground troops while these honorable soldiers drive west. We will have sixteen dive bombers for this sortie. I will lead one flight of the Aichi ninety-nine bombers to attack Anamo and Lieutenant Kurosawa will attack Afua with the other flight of Aichis. Lieutenant Muto will mount twelve Mitsubishi fighters as our escort, for we can expect the Americans to have their own aircraft over the Aitape area this morning.''

"There may be swarms of American fighters, captain," Lieutenant Muto said. "I do not know if we can protect the bombers with a mere twelve Mitsubishi fighters."

"If you can hold off enemy interceptors long enough for us to make our dive bombing runs, you can consider your mission a success," the captain said.

"We will do our best," Muto answered.

"Ground crews are now pre-flighting our bombers and fighters. We will leave Boram at 0615 hours to make our strikes at about 0645 hours. Any questions?"

None.

"Good," Akamatsu nodded, "then let us man our aircraft, and may the Heavenly spirits guide us to a successful mission."

At 0615, Capt. Sadaaki Akamatsu zoomed down the Boram runway with his wingman before they hoisted their Val dive bombers into the air. Soon, 14 more Vals were also airborne. Moments later, Lt. Sadao Muto led his 12 Zero fighters down the same Boram runway before he too left the Wewak airdrome. By 0630, the 248th Flying Regiment was already halfway to Aitape.

Like Maj. Tom McGuire of the U.S. 431st Fighter Squadron, Lieutenant Muto also kept fighter planes far in the van to keep an eye out for enemy interceptors.

At 0615 hours, July 11, in the U.S. base at Anamo on the north coast of Aitape, Gen. William Gill met with Col. Bob Fowler, CO of the 128th Regiment, and with Lt. Col. Henry Geebs, CO of the 128th's 2nd Battalion. Geebs had come up from Chinapelli to take over 2nd Battalion, leaving his E and H Companies under Capt. Herman Botcher.

"C Company is cut off and in danger of annihilation," Gill said, "while the Japanese are probably strengthening defenses in their captured pocket west of the Driniumor. I'd guess they're anchoring themselves to push us out of Chinapelli. If we lose that village, the Koronal and X-ray Rivers' defenses will be exposed. Meanwhile, the Nips are no doubt pouring more troops westward."

"We've got an air strike from two groups coming in at about 0645 hours," Colonel Howe said.

"I know," General Gill said. "Still, I'd like to coordinate a ground attack with a second air strike. I've asked V Bomber Command in Hollandia to ready another attack late this morning in conjunction with a ground counter attack."

"A counter attack, sir?" Lt. Colonel Geebs asked.

"The 2nd Battalion, colonel," Gillis said. "They've been over the terrain from the Driniumor River defenses to Anamo. You'll have both F and G Company with you and these men know the trails. You'll have two missions: break up any enemy positions and relieve the trapped C Company. Do you think you can do it?"

"I'll do it," Geebs said.

"I'll call Hollandia and ask for the second air strike for 1100 hours. Do you think you can be in position to attack the Japs by then?"

"Yes sir," Geebs said.

"We'll furnish as much artillery as we can," the 32nd Infantry Division commander said.

Meanwhile, the 3rd and 475th Groups droned east southeast, while the Japanese 248th Flying Regiment droned west northwest. At 0635 hours, Capt. Perry Dahl, one of the two U.S. fighter pilots on scout spotted the Japanese planes and he quickly called Maj. Tom McGuire.

"Bandits coming from the southeast! Bandits!"

"Okay, let's move after them," McGuire answered. The major then called MacDonald. "Bandits up ahead, colonel. We don't know how many, but we'll intercept."

"Goddamn," the 475th commander cursed. He had no choice now but to release another of his squadrons to help the 431st against the enemy planes. He called the squadron leader of

185

the 432nd. "Captain, salvo your bombs and join Major McGuire against those bandits coming in from the southeast."

"Roger," the captain answered.

Soon, 32 Lightning pilots zoomed after the oncoming enemy planes.

To the south, the van scouts of the 248th Flying Regiment had also spotted the American aircraft and they quickly called Lt. Sadao Muto. "Enemy aircraft to the northwest, Honorable Muto; swarms of them."

"We must stop them," Muto said. "The Aichi dive bombers cannot be deterred from their mission."

But, the ensuing clash became a lopsided massacre. McGuire took the 475th's 431st Squadron after the Japanese Zeros, while the 432nd Squadron salvoed its bombs and took after the Japanese Val dive bombers. The 32 American fighter pilots waded into the 248th formation like fierce, marauding hawks. Lieutenant Muto tried desperately to hold off the Lightnings, but the Zeros were inferior to the P-38 fighter planes, and Muto's pilots lacked the experience and training of the U.S. pilots. The slow moving Val dive bombers, with a single gunner and mere twin 7.7mm guns, offered little challenge to the six spitting .50 caliber wing guns of the P-38s.

McGuire himself quickly tailed a Zero and blew the plane apart with a shattering stream of tracer fire. A moment later, he caught a second

Zero in his sights and chopped off the tail with ripping .50 caliber fire before the Zero cartwheeled into the jungle and exploded. Capt. Perry Dahl dove on a Zero and ripped off the Mitsubishi's wing before the plane flipped over and dropped into the jungle like a huge, dead albatross. Other U.S. pilots also scored heavily against the Japanese fighter planes, downing five more Zeros and damaging others.

Lt. Sadao Muto called off the dogfight and roared eastward with a mere four remaining planes, two of which were damaged. In the fleeting moments of battle the Zero fighter unit had suffered near disaster, while the Americans did not lose a single P-38, although two Lightnings had suffered damage.

Now without escorts, Captain Akamatsu's Vals became easy prey for the pilots of the 432nd Fighter Squadron. The U.S. pilots tore into one Val after another, chopping off wings, knocking off tails, destroying engines, or ripping apart fuselages with .50 caliber fire. Vals blew up in mid air, cartwheeled to oblivion, tumbled into the sea, or crashed in the jungles.

Within two minutes, Captain Akamatsu had lost eight of his 16 planes and he frantically called off the mismatch. "We must return to Wewak. There are too many enemy fighter planes."

But before the Vals got away, the Americans shot down two more of the dive bombers and damaged another pair. Thus, in the swift engagement, the 248th Flying Regiment had lost 18 of its 28 planes, with other damaged. The Vals had not dropped a single bomb on American positions at Afua or at Anamo.

Meanwhile, free of Zero interference, Lt. Col. Dick Ellis led his A-20s in a sweep over the Japanese positions. The Havoc light bombers roared over the trees with blistering strafing fire from six .50 caliber nose guns. The A-20s released countless clusters of frag bombs and dozens of 100 pound demo bombs into the thick brakes. The jungle shook violently from the staccato of explosions that felled trees, chopped away heavy branches, scattered green folliage like confetti, and chased off squealing tropical birds in panic. The 3rd Group airmen left a pall of smoke rising out of the jungle.

South of the A-20 targets, Lt. Col. Charles MacDonald led his P-58 fighter-bombers. Again, American planes sent streams of .50 caliber fire into the brakes before releasing clusters of parafrags and whistling 100 pounders. Once more, smoke and fire rose from the jungle.

"Okay," Ellis cried into his radio, "let's go home."

"Roger, Dick," MacDonald answered.

The Americans soon droned north northwest, certain they had pulverized the enemy positions to thwart the 18th Army offensive. But, the foxy Japanese had not been badly hurt by the low level air attacks.

General Miyake had wisely ignored the pleas of some of his subordinates to continue the offensive after the two victories on the night of July 10-11. The Aitape Assault Force commander had fought the Americans too long in these jungles of New Guinea and he knew too well the power of the U.S. 5th Air Force. Thus, correctly, he had put his troops to work building strong bunkers. The effort had paid off. The clusters of 28 pound parafrags had done little damage to the sheltered supplies or troops who had burrowed themselves into their log covered holes. Even the 100 pound bombs had caused few casualties, except in the case of some direct hits. And finally, the heavy strafing fire had merely popped up clods of earth or punched holes in the coconut logs that covered the shelters.

When the U.S. air attacks ended, General Miyake quickly organized work parties to snuff out fires and to clear away debris in the blasted jungle forests. He then called his unit commander into a quick conference.

"What it the damage?" the general asked.

"Only minor in our sector," Colonel Matsumoto of the 78th Infantry said. "We lost twelve men killed and another dozen wounded. Only a few boxes of supplies were destroyed."

"And you, colonel?" Miyake looked at Tsuji.

"Two of our trenches were annihilated with eight men lost," Tsuji answered. "My battalion is still at near full strength. We lost only a few supplies in the air attacks."

"Good, good," Miyake nodded vigorously. "Keep your men sheltered for the remainder of the day. The enemy may conduct more attacks during daylight. We will continue our advance at dusk."

"Yes, Honorable Miyake."

Miyake then looked at the 237th Regiment commander. "Colonel, you will advance on Anamo with elements of your coastal force, perhaps during the dark hours you can attack and overrun them."

"Yes, Honorable general," Masahuko Nara answered.

Miyake then looked at Colonel Matsumoto. "You will send a battalion of your seventy-eighth Regiment to attack Afua to the south. Meanwhile, I would ask that you send your First Battalion to cross the Driniumor River south of Afua to attack the American force from the rear. The pincer will either destroy the enemy defenders at Afua or force them into a quick withdrawal. Your operation, Colonel Matsumoto, and that of Colonel Nara will protect our flanks while the remainder of our troops march westward to capture Palauru and Chinapelli."

For the next hour, the Japanese cleared the debris left by American bombs. However, they soon sheltered themselves again as a dozen Beaufort light bombers and a dozen P-40s of the RAAF 70 Wing hit the 18th Army positions with strafing fire and 100 pound bombs. But the Australians only did minimal damage.

Then at about 0800 hours, a scout hurried into the Japanese ADVON headquarters of the Aitape Assault Force to see the general. "Honorable Miyake," the runner said, "a strong enemy force is coming south from Anamo. They apparently hope to relieve their trapped company of men and perhaps attack our north flank."

"How far are they?"

"Perhaps five miles."

"You have done well," Miyake told the scout. "Get some food and rest." Miyake turned to an aide. Get me Colonel Nara, Major Yamashita, and Major Hoshimo."

"Yes, general, at once."

Within moments, the subordinates were in Miyake's tent. "An enemy force is coming southward. Colonel, you will dispatch your First Battalion northward at once to dispose of this American unit." He then looked at Hoshimo. "Is it possible that we can send artillery to aid Major Yamashita in this endeavor?"

Hoshimo grinned. "We have not been idle, Honorable Miyake. We already have most of our big guns disassembled and ready to pack on horses. Yes, we can send 75mm guns northward with Major Yamashita's First Battalion."

"You will dispatch six guns."

"Yes, general," Hoshimo said.

Meanwhile, Capt. George Royce had received

word from Anamo that help was on the way to relieve his C Company. Lt. Col. Henry Geebs was coming south out of the coastal town with 400 men of his 2nd Battalion, 128th Infantry, to break the Japanese siege. As soon as Royce got this encouraging message he talked to his officers.

"I want a platoon on the north to keep the enemy pinned down. As soon as Colonel Geebs comes within striking distance, we'll attack those Nips around our positions. If we get those Japanese troops in a crossfire, we can either destroy them or chase them off. Who's dug in on the north flank?"

"Sgt. Gerry Endl and First Platoon."

"Okay, tell him to prepare for a fire fight."

"Yes sir."

When Endl got word of the relief column moving southward, he quickly called together his squad sergeants. "Help is on the way; a whole battalion from the One-twenty-eighth Infantry. Make sure your rifles, machine gun, and mortar teams are on full alert. As soon as the column is close enough, we'll hit the Nips to our north."

"Okay, Gerry," one of the squad sergeants said.

Unfortunately, before Lt. Col. Henry Geebs and his 2nd Battalion troops reached the entrapped C Company, and before a new 5th Air Force attack, Maj. Tadi Yamashita had arrived at a point north of the trapped American soldiers. Yamashita's battalion arrived with their six artillery guns and at 1030 hours Nippon scouts had spotted the Americans—before U.S. scouts sighted the Japanese.

"Honorable Yamashita, the enemy force is about a kilometer ahead of us."

"Then we will stop here," Yamashita said. "We will assemble the artillery pieces at once and attack them. Do you know their exact position?"

"Yes," the scout said. "I can tell you where to direct artillery and mortar fire, where to emplace snipers in the trees, and where to set up machine guns."

"Good, good," the major nodded.

Within a few minutes, the Japanese had completed their work to meet the oncoming Americans. Capt. Kazuo Sugino, Lt. Toshishige Onizuka, Sgt. Kiyoshi Itoh, and other officers and non-coms quickly placed men into ambush positions. By 1045 hours, the Japanese were ready. Yamashita waited until the Americans came within 200 yards before he gave the order to open fire with 75mm cannon and 90mm mortar.

Geeb's troops had moved warily through the jungle, with Captain Fulmer's G Company in the lead and keeping scouts to the van. The Americans however, had not spotted the Japanese; nor would they since Yamashita's troops and guns were now well concealed in the dense jungle foliage. In fact, the GIs of the 2nd

Battalion had almost relaxed when the numbing explosions burst into their midst.

Deafening concussions and fiery orange balls erupted in the thick brush. Limbs snapped, tree trunks toppled, foliage scattered, and American GIs suffered bloody, instant death. Arms, legs, and torsos flew in a dozen directions.

"Take cover! Cover!" Lt. Col. Geebs cried.

The GIs scattered as more whooshing 75mm artillery and 90mm mortar shells ripped through the jungle to kill and injure GIs. The deadly barrage had continued for a full two minutes amidst the screams of dying U.S. infantrymen. All around him, Geebs saw the battered bodies of the dead and the moaning wounded who flopped about the damp jungle floor like injured cougars.

Geebs finally gave the order: "Pull back! Pull back! They've got those big guns again. Pull back!"

"How the hell did they get those pieces in here?" Captain Fulmer cried. "How the hell can they do it?"

"I don't know," Geebs answered, "but they're tearing us apart. Pull back," the 2nd Battalion commander said again.

As before, relatively calm non-coms like Sgt. Henry Cooper kept panic at a minimun as they directed the horrified GIs through the dense jungles and to safety. Finally, at about 1100 hours, the U.S. battalion had moved out of Japanese artillery and mortar range. However, they had left behind 20 dead, although they had carried off their some 40 wounded men. The battered GIs of 2nd Battalion plodded back towards Anamo, their bodies drained and exhausted from the brutal big gun attack.

"Shall we pursue these Yankee dogs?" Captain Sugino asked Major Yamashita.

"Not now," Yamashita grinned. "Our troops will rest for the remainder of the day and we will join other units of Hara's Coastal Force to attack the enemy in his positions at Anamo tonight. The lieutenant colonel then squinted upwards to peek at the few patches of skylight that filtered through the dense foliage. "Be sure the men are well scattered and deeply sheltered in trenches. We may expect more enemy air attacks."

"Yes, major," Captain Sugino said.

Yamashita was right. Both the 3rd Bomb Group and the 475th Fighter Group were droning towards the Driniumor River battle area for another air attack. The U.S. airmen would arrive too late to help the tattered U.S. 2nd Battalion.

Chapter Eleven

Lt. Col. Richard Ellis reached the Aitape area with 42 Havocs at 1115 hours to conduct his next strafing and bombing run over the Japanese positions. Right behind the 3rd Group aircraft came 40 Lightnings of the 475th Fighter Group to make their own strafing and bombing runs. This time, they met no enemy planes. As the 5th Air Force aircraft passed over Tadji, Ellis called the ADVON Percussion headquarters.

"Where do you want us to strike?"

"You're a little late, colonel," somebody answered. "Those bastards had their big artillery again and they forced our ground troops to pull back to Anamo with considerable losses."

"Where are those Nips? We'll send one squadron to hit them, while the rest of us hit their main positions around the Driniumor."

"If you look at your map, it's at coordinate 134.1 by 6.72."

"Okay," Ellis said. He called Ken Rosebush. "Major, take your Ninetieth Squadron and lay a carpet attack on this coordinate: 134.1 by 6.72.

Have you got that on your chart?"

"I've got it, colonel. Will do."

"The rest of us are going on to those positions we hit earlier," the 3rd Group commander said. He then called Lt. Colonel MacDonald of the 475th Group. "Charlie, I've dispatched one of my squadrons to hit a forward enemy position, so we'll have to spread out a little to hit the primary Driniumor targets."

"I thought our targests were further north to support ground units?"

"It didn't work out," Ellis said. "The GIs met too much opposition, especially from heavy artillery and heavy mortar."

"Goddamn it," MacDonald cursed.

The Japanese, long accustomed to heavy U.S. 5th Air Force aerial attacks, had taken precautions against air strikes. In fact, protection for air attacks had become a part of any Japanese strategy, defense or offense. General Miyake's main body still remained in their log covered holes, whole Maj. Tadi Yamashita, after driving back the U.S. 2nd Battalion, had quickly scattered his 1st Battalion. He ordered his men to dig holes and shelter themselves from possible air attacks.

Yamashita had completed his defense efforts by the time the zooming A-20s of the 3rd Group's 90th Squadron roared over the jungle and spit .50 caliber machine gun fire, dropped clusters of parafrags, and unleashed 100 pound demo bombs. The jungle shook for the aerial assault, as bombs chopped holes in the terrain, toppled some of the smaller trees, and sent limbs thumping to earth. But the Japanese 1st Battalion suffered few casualties, with less than a dozen men killed and perhaps 20 wounded.

Similarly, the major aerial assault on the Aitape Assault Force also caused minimal losses in dead, wounded, and supplies. The three squadrons of A-20s came in first at low level, followed by the P-38s of the 475th Group. Chattering nose and wing guns erupted countless pops of earth, split tree branches, and scattered brush. Descending clusters of parafrags exploded in staccato bursts, and 100 pound demo bombs erupted in numbing concussions. Once more the U.S. airmen left a huge square of fire and smoke in their wake, but again, the Americans had not caused serious losses.

By mid afternoon of July 11, Lt. Col. Henry Geebs and his plodding GIs had marched halfway back to Anamo, with medics helping wounded along the way. During a ten minute break, Sgt. Henry Cooper and Cpl. Joe Cartwright sat against a tree to drink water from a canteen, while they wiped perspiration from their faces.

"Goddamn it, Hank," Cartwright said, "this thing is unreal. First, we nearly get the shit kicked out of us on those river defenses and now they cut us to pieces with heavy artillery in the middle of this fuckin' jungle. How come they can be so strong? They don't have any more troops than we have."

"They're tenacious sons 'a bitches," Cooper said. "They do things in this jungle that no human should be able to do, and their big artillery pieces gave them an edge. I'll never know how they get that cannon into this bush. And they may not be finished," the sergeant gestured. "They're kickin' the hell out of us and they've got the initiative. Even if we get back to Anamo without any more trouble, those Nip bastards will likely be right on our ass."

Cpl. Cartwright shook his head. "Our fly boys hit 'em twice this morning and I know they're comin' back this afternoon. Christ, we own the air over this jungle, and they bomb the hell out of those Nips. How come they still boot us around?"

"Because they're like moles," Sgt. Cooper said. "They just bury themselves in the ground and those goddamn bombs and tracer fire don't touch 'em. When an air strike is over, they crawl out of their holes and fight some more, and mostly at night when our flyboys can't do anything. Those Nips got no food, no medicine, no nothing, but still they fight like demons."

"We'll get them, though," Corporal Cartwright said. "We got 'em at Buna, we got 'em at Finchhaven, and we got 'em at Saidor. We'll get the bastards here, too." The corporal took another gulp from his canteen and then poured some of the water over his face, hot and sweating from the steaming, humid jungle.

"Jesus, I wish I was in Siberia right now where I could roll in the snow. This humidity and these goddamn bugs are driving me crazy."

"You ought to be used to them by now," Cooper grinned.

"Maybe they'll send us back to Australia for a rest when this thing is over," Cartwright said. "Christ, they can't let us rot in these jungles forever."

"First we gotta push back those Nips," Cooper said, "and that won't be easy, the way they've shoved us around. I think we'll have to get cannon in here, too, if we're gonna do that." The platoon sergeant then looked at his men and scowled. The GIs lay haphazardly on the damp jungle floor. They were tired, exhausted, and relishing every second of this ten minute break. "I feel sorry for those guys," Cooper cocked his head towards the dogfaces.

"They'll make out," Cartwright said. "They learn to live with this climate; the insects, the sweat, and the Nips. They'll make it."

Elsewhere, Lt. Colonel Geebs spoke to Capt. Tally Fulmer. "We're about three miles from Anamo, but we'll need to keep moving."

"The men are spent, colonel," Fulmer said. "They don't have the strength to go much further."

"They better find the strength," Geebs huffed. "If those Nips are behind us, they're probably dragging those heavy guns with them. They could hurt us again."

"Are we sure they're following us?" Captain Fulmer asked. "We haven't seen a sign of them. We've had no reports on them from our rear scouts."

"When did you ever see those bastards in the jungle before they hit us?" the 2nd Battalion commander answered. "No, we can't rest too long." Geebs looked at his watch. "Okay, the break's over. Let's mount up."

"Yes sir," Captain Fulmer said.

Soon, the cry from non-coms echoed through the jungles. "Mount up! Mount up! We're moving out!"

Within a few minutes, the nearly 400 men of the 2nd Battalion's two companies were again plodding through the jungle. They once more struggled through deep brush, often using bolos to cut their way ahead. They slogged over muddy terrain and sloshed through swift streams, always swatting the swarms of insects and bugs that buzzed about their faces like tenacious bees after nectar. Or the GIs continually wiped the perspiration from their faces, necks, and arms, while their green fatigue uniforms hung on them like damp, heavy rags from the incessant perspiration that headed every pore in their itching bodies—from the top of their heads to their sore feet.

Lt. Colonel Geebs, himself nearly 40 years old, would not slow the men down because he wanted to reach the defense perimeter at Anamo before the Japanese could swarm over them in the black evening like demons rising out of hell. Capt. Bob Seely of F Company and Capt. Tally Fulmer of G Company felt bitter. They had been on the line for a long time; their companies had been forced to retreat from the Driniumor, with G Company almost getting overrun. Now they had been sent back into the jungle again this morning only to take another lacing from the Japanese with heavy casualties. They should have been relieved, but they were still fighting the Japanese in this miserable jungle.

Since midnight last night, the Jungle Lizards of the 32nd Division had taken a battering from the enemy. They had suffered enough from the Japanese 18th Army and why didn't they hurry up with the those 124th Regiment reinforcements? The only consolation for Captains Seely and Fulmer was that they arrived at Anamo about dusk, in time for them to at least enjoy a hot meal.

But deep in the jungle, C Company was still trapped in its pocket. With the withdrawal of 2nd Battalion, the men feared the worst. As the afternoon passed, Sgt. Gerry Endl squinted up at the waning daylight, hoping the day would not end. He knew the Japanese strategy was obviously to attack at night. In fact, the men of Endl's platoon had eaten their evening meal of K ration early to prepare themselves for the worst—a possible overwhelming banzai charge from all sides during the height of the jungle darkness. At dusk, Endl met with Capt. George

Royce and other officers and non-coms of C Company.

"How are supplies?" Royce asked.

"Most of the men are down to a couple of cartons of K rations, sir," Sergeant Endl said. "By this time tomorrow we'll be out."

"Goddamn it," Royce cursed. "Didn't we bring out any rations with us?"

"There wasn't time," Endl said.

"How about ammunition?"

"My own platoon has about 100 rounds per man and maybe a half dozen grenades per man," the platoon sergeant said.

"That's not a hell of a lot," Royce scowled. "Maybe we could beat off one banzai charge, but after that—" He screwed his face and studied his subordinates before he continued. "Our men need to be well dug in, and they've got to make every shot count if those Japs attack tonight."

"What about relief?" a lieutenant asked. "Will they try again?"

"I don't know," Royce said.

"Can we sneak our way out of this trap?" another officer asked.

"I don't know that either," the captain answered, "but that may be our only chance. If we get hit hard, we'll have to make a break no matter how many casualties we suffer. The alternative might be a wipe-out."

"Can I send out scouts, sir, to see if the Nips have any weak spots where we might break out?'' Sergeant Endl asked.

"That's a good idea, sergeant," Royce nodded. "You have my permission." Then the captain sighed and looked at his officers and non-coms. "Okay, get back to your platoon and squads. Keep the men fully alert."

"Yes sir," somebody answered.

Fortunately for Captain Royce, the Japanese had more elaborate plans for the moment, and they elected not to concern themselves with a mere company of trapped American soldiers. Gen. Sadahiko Miyake was content to keep the C Company GIs cowering and nervous in their surrounded perimeter, while the Aitape Attack Force moved onto more important gains. At dusk, July 12, Miyake called his commanders into conference at his jungle headquarters.

"We will make another attack tonight."

"The Coastal Force is ready, general," Colonel Nara said. "Major Yamashita is even now within a mile of Anamo and the remainder of our force will be there within a few hours. Major Hoshimo is moving big cannon up the Afua-Anamo Trail and by midnight we should have a dozen 75mm guns for the assault on Anamo."

"Good," Miyake nodded. He then looked at Colonel Ide. "What of the Eightieth Regiment?"

"We too are prepared to march, Honorable Miyake," Colonel Ide answered. "Lt. Colonel Tsuji has already left with the Second Battalion as a vanguard force and his troops should reach

204

the enemy defenses at Chinapelli well before midnight. The other Eightieth Infantry Battalions will be at Palauru shortly before midnight. By dawn, I expect to occupy both villages. We will then dig into a new perimeter."

"Will it not be difficult for your troops to push through seven or eight miles of jungle in so short a time?" Miyake asked.

"Our troops are eager, general," Ide said. "They have finally tasted victory after so many months of defeat. They will stop at nothing; not the aerial bombardments, not the incessant insects, the stifling himidity, the thick brush, or the eerie jungle darkness. I have heard only cheers from my troops when I told them we might continue our drive westward this evening."

"I am pleased," the Aitape Assault Force commander said. "I will assign at least six of the 75mm cannon to your unit." Miyake then looked at Col. Mitsujiro Matsumoto. "What of your Seventy-eighth Regiment?"

Colonel Matsumoto grinned. "Our First Battalion has already crossed the Driniumor River south of Afua. They will begin a march northward against Afua as soon as they receive word from me. Meanwhile, the remainder of my troops are prepared to move south as soon as you give the order."

"A company of Major Hoshimo's artillery troops will accompany you with ten 75mm guns, I am told," Miyake said.

"Excellent," Matsumoto said. "These cannon will make a difference."

Miyake nodded and then squinted up at the darkening sky. "Let us hope that when sunlight emerges again above these jungle trees we have captured our objectives—Anamo to the north, Chinapelli and Palauru to the west, and Afua to the south. I suggest, gentlemen, that you begin your marches at once so we can conduct simultaneous assaults at about midnight."

"Yes, Honorable Miyake," Colonel Ide said.

At the same early evening, Col. Robert Fowler checked his 128th Regiment positions at Anamo on the coast. The 1st Battalion, minus the trapped C Company and Geebs' battered companies of 2nd Battalion had dug themselves in at the coastal village. Fowler spread out his machine gun crews, mortar teams, light 37mm artillery men, BAR units, and rifle squads in a semicircle around Anamo. The colonel also alerted the desron commander of the American destroyers offshore to use 5″ warship guns if such support became necessary.

At 1800 hours, Fowler met with Lt. Colonel Geebs. "I know your battalion has suffered a lot, Henry, but we may get new banzai charges tonight. Those Nips that hit your battalion this morning may be a vanguard of a whole Japanese regiment moving on Anamo. And, if they have that heavy artillery with them, we could have a rough time."

"What about our own guns?" Geebs asked.

"Hell, they ought to be able to bring them to Anamo by LCI's or even LCM's."

"I've asked for 155mm artillery," Fowler said, "and General Gill said a battery was on the way to Anamo."

"But will we have them to fight tonight?" Geebs scowled.

"I hope so," Fowler said. "In any case, make sure your men are ready."

"Yes sir."

But, Lt. Col. Henry Geebs felt no confidence; nor did Captain Seely of the battalion's F Company, nor Captain Fulmer of G Company. If the Japanese hit again, they would begin with stealthy infiltrations through the dense jungles to disrupt communications and cause panic among the GIs before they launched their banzai charges.

To the west, Col. Merle Howe and the combined H and E Company had established defense positions at the village of Chinapelli and Palauru on the west bank of the X-ray River. Howe had just finished evening mess and then spoken to his executive officer, Maj. Joseph Mainz.

"Are we dug in?"

"Yes sir," the major answered. "We're got a two hundred yard line on the river bank, with at least a dozen machine gun posts and several mortar pits. The men are pretty well rested and just waiting."

"Good," Howe nodded. "We'll have to be

alert. I got an idea the Japanese will hit us sometime after midnight. They won't be content to sit on their cans along the Driniumor.''

"Do you think they'll have that 75mm cannon with them?" Mainz asked.

"Maybe."

"You mean they can drag those guns all the way here from the Driniumor?"

"I don't know how they do it, but they do," the colonel shook his head.

"I sure wish we had some of those 205's back in Tadji," the major said.

"The jungle trails from the Nigia River are too narrow," Howe said. Then he sighed. "If they hit us in heavy force again, we'll simply have to retire to the Nigia River defenses."

"Yes sir," Major Mainz said.

To the south, at Afua, Capt. Leonard Lowry of the Lowry Force met with Lt. Col. Peter Hooper, commander of the 112th Cavalry Regiment. "Have you deployed your two companies along the river, captain?"

"Yes sir," Lowry said. "I've got K Company on the south and my own I Company on the north. We'll do what we can to hold off any new assaults." Then the captain screwed his face. "Do you think we'll get more attacks tonight?"

"That seems to be the pattern," Hooper said. "If they come in force, we'll have a rough time. I've only got two reinforced companies here, I Troop to the north and F Troop to the south. If the Nips come from the north, I'll send F Troop to help out, and if they come across the river, I'll send F Troop to help out your two companies."

"What if they come from both directions like they did last night?"

"We can hold off a couple of battalions," Lt. Colonel Hooper said, "unless they bring that big artillery with them again. We've only got 37mm guns and 51mm mortar. I suggest you have your men set up more barbed wire fences along that river bank."

"I'll do that, colonel."

Hooper nodded. "All we can do now is hope for the best."

For the tense Americans, the witching hour came again at midnight on the evening of July 11-12. By 2400, the Coastal Force under Col. Masahuka Nara had reached the stretch of jungle before Anamo. He had with him a dozen 75mm guns that Maj. Iwataro Hoshimo had remarkably brought up through the jungles in dismantled parts on the backs of horses. At the same hour, Col. Takutoro Ide had reached the X-ray River area with two battalions of troops from his 80th Regiment to attack Chinapelli and Palauru. And finally, Col. Mitsujiro Matsumoto had established his pincer around Afua, with one battalion to the south and an artillery supported battalion on the north.

Shortly after midnight, July 12, the Japanese unloosed mortar and artillery barrages into the dark, silent jungle. The whooshing shells exploded into American positions with deafening dins and blinding flashes. American GIs cowered in their trenches—at Anamo, at Afua, and on the X-Ray River. The Japanese were conducting a replay of last night and now they were attacking on three fronts. Once more the screams and moans of dying and wounded GIs challenged the sounds of bursting shells; and once more American soldiers waited fearfully for the banzai charges that were sure to come. The Americans responded to the heavy cannonades with 37mm cannon and 51mm mortar but these were no match for the 75mm artillery barrels and 90mm mortar tubes. Even the 5″ and 3″ naval guns from the U.S. destroyers had failed to deter the Japanese.

And even worse, Nippon infiltrators had sneaked into American positions in every area to cut communications or to lob grenades into many of the American foxholes and trenches. The infiltrators had caused panic among the American troops and seriously hurt their ability to maintain a strong, organized defense against the assailants.

In the north, after the artillery and mortar barrage, and despite the U.S. naval gunfire from offshore, the first waves of ground troops from Colonel Nara's Coastal Force rushed foreward into the American positions at Anamo.

"Banzai! Banzai! Banzai!"

Hordes of Japanese fell before withering machine gun fire, BAR, and rifle fire, and many of the Nippon jungle fighters disappeared in 5″

naval bursts. But the waves came on from the dense trees until some of Nara's troops overran the American perimeter. Col. Robert Fowler had no choice but to abandon the coastal village. He ordered a retreat westward along the coastal trail, leaving behind some 25 dead. And, although his own GIs had killed more than 200 of the attacking Japanese, the enemy soon occupied Anamo.

Colonel Nara stood on the shoreline, looked out to sea, and grinned in elation. "We have won our objective."

"Our losses were heavy, colonel," Captain Sugino answered soberly.

"It is the price one must pay for victory," Nara answered. "You will order your troops to dig in quickly in strength. We can expect enemy air attacks at daylight, and perhaps even bombardment from the sea."

"Yes, Honorable Nara," Sugino answered, "I will instruct Sergeant Itoh at once."

On the west, with Lt. Col. Masanasobu Tsuji's 2nd Battalion leading the way, the 80th Infantry Regiment under Col. Tokutaro Ide breached the American defenses at the X-ray River. After the heavy 75mm and 90mm mortar barrages, the Japanese launched massive banzai charges over the stream. The assault forced Col. Merle Howe to abandon his X-ray River defenses. Howe led his GIs swiftly to the westward through the jungles, plodding as far as he could to reach the U.S. secondary defenses on

211

the Nigia River. By 0200 hours, Lt. Colonel Tsuji was sitting in Colonel Howe's deserted headquarters tent. The 80th Regiment troops had captured both Chinapelli and Palauru.

To the south, at Afua, the Japanese conducted the same artillery-banzai assault as had Colonel Nara and Colonel Ide at Anamo and on the X-ray River. The overwhelming Nippon attack, for both north and south, with booming 75mm artillery and 90mm mortar support, forced Lt. Col. Peter Hooper to abandon Afua. He withdrew westward with his own troopers and the two companies from Lowry Force. By 0100 hours, July 12, Col. Mitsujiro Matsumoto and his victorious soldiers of the 78th Regiment occupied Afua. Matsumoto had surely atoned for his defeat on that first assault across the Driniumor River 25 hours ago.

"Banzai! Banzai! Banzai! Banzai!" The elated cries from the 78th Regiment jungle fighters echoed through the dark jungles in an incessant cadence. Colonel Matsumoto made no attempt to stop his frenzied soldiers for they had earned this moment of celebration.

Thus had the night of July 11-12 proved as disastrous to the Americans as had the evening of July 10-11. In the north, the battered U.S. 128th Regiment had retired to the river at the delta of the Koronal River. In the center, Colonel Howe's 127th Regiment troops had not stopped until they reached the west bank of the Nigia River, leaving Chinapelli and Palauru firmly in Japanese hands. In the south the 112th Cavalry troopers and the Lowry Force had retreated westward toward the X-ray River and continued their withdrawal to the opposite bank of this river.

By dawn of July 12, the Japanese forward elements under Lt. Colonel Tsuji firmly entrenched themselves less than five miles from the Tadji airdromes. But, once more, like vampires who hid from the fatal brightness of daylight, the Japanese disappeared into their holes to wait out potentially fatal air attacks in daylight.

Without doubt, the Americans were in serious trouble. Gen. William Gill, commander of the 32nd Infantry Division, now realized a sobering truth. He matched the Japanese in numbers of troops and he enjoyed air support. But he lacked the heavy artillery in the depths of the jungle that had given the enemy a tremendous advantage. Gill sat glumly in his field headquarters, wondering how he could stop further advances by the Japanese; wondering if the enemy would push on again when darkness returned to the New Guinea jungle.

In contrast, Gen. Hatazo Adachi wallowed in delight when he heard of these new successes. "We have finally extracted vengeance against these Jungle Lizards. Now it is they who will suffer the agony of death and retreat."

And indeed, the Jungle Lizards of the U.S. 32nd Red Arrow Division fully expected a new assault from their old enemy—the Japanese 18th Army.

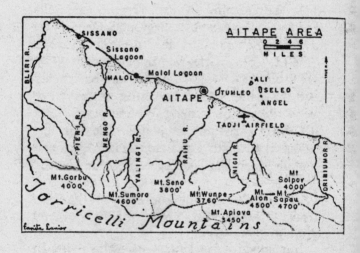

The Aitape area with its important Tadji airfield and
Driniumor River to right

Chapter Twelve

On the morning of July 12, U.S. air units returned to the Aitape battleground. Once more, Lt. Col. Dick Ellis led his 3rd Group's A-20s, while Lt. Col. Charles MacDonald led his 475th Group's P-38s. Maj. Tom McGuire once again used the group's 431st Squadron in the van to keep alert for enemy interceptors. But McGuire's P-38s met no planes. The Japanese had less than a half dozen aircraft in Wewak and Captain Akamutsu was in no position to send anything west. Despite his pleas to the 4th Air Army and despite the successes of the 18th Army, General Teramoto would not send Akamutsu any aircraft.

At 0640 hours, McGuire called Ellis. "It's all clear up ahead, colonel."

"Roger," Ellis answered. He then called Mac-Donald. "Charlie, we'll take Anamo and the Koronal River sectors. You take Afua and the X-ray River areas to the south."

"Okay, Dick," MacDonald answered.

Again the Japanese had spent the dark hours

of early morning to shelter themselves in their newly won positions. In the north, Colonel Nara's Coastal Force, the 237th Infantry and attached 41st Artillery, had dug in deeply in and around Anamo. In the center, Colonel Ide had burrowed his 80th Regiment soldiers in and around the villages of Chinapelli and Palauru, with Lt. Colonel Tsuji's 2nd Battalion entrenched along the X-ray River. To the south, Colonel Matsumoto's 78th Regiment had excavated foxholes in the Afua area and along the southern length of the X-ray River.

The Japanese now remained hidden to wait out the air attacks, while supplies came over the jungle trails or along the coast from Wewak. General Miyake had planned another multiple attack tonight. He hoped to cross the X-ray and Koronal Rivers to storm through the American defenses on the Nigia River, the last obstacle to the Tadji airdromes and Aitape itself.

At 0700 hours, the first whistling bombs from the 3rd Group's 8th Squadron sailed into the Anamo area, erupting numbing explosions and several fires. Then came the A-20s of the group's 13th Squadron that ignited more fires. By the time the two squadrons zoomed away from the coastal area, a blanket of smoke had enveloped a huge patch of terrain.

"Goddamn it," Ellis said, "if we didn't get the bastards this time, we'll never get them."

In the center, Maj. Ken Rosebush led the 90th Squadron over the villages of Chinapelli and

Palauru, sending dozens of 100 pound demolition bombs and hundreds of .50 caliber strafing rounds into the area. The 90th left the two villages afire and flattened. Behind Rosebush came the 3rd's 89th Squadron which raked the west shoreline of the X-ray River with more 100 pounders and .50 caliber strafing fire.

By 0710 hours, the A-20 attack was over. As the Havocs veered away, Ken Rosebush studied the widespread patch of smoke and called Ellis. "We must have slaughtered those Nips this time, colonel."

"Maybe," the 3rd Group commander answered.

To the south, MacDonald zoomed over the Afua area with his 432nd and 433rd Squadrons of the 475th Fighter Group. The P-38s sent 100 pound demo bombs into targets and erupted dozens of explosions that felled trees, snapped huge branches, and started numerous fires. The P-38s then returned on strafing runs. Meanwhile, Tom McGuire and his pilots of the 431st Squadron zoomed at treetop level along the west bank of the X-ray River to attack suspected Japanese positions. The Lightnings left a length of fire and smoke along the river and McGuire was satisfied. He called his pilots.

"We can't do anything more here; let's go home."

"Okay, major," one of the pilots answered.

By 0730 hours, the 3rd Group A-20s and 475th Group P-38s were gone, soaring back to

Hollandia. Less than a half hour later, Beauforts and P-40s of the RAAF 70 Wing attacked the Japanese positions with raking .50 caliber strafing fire and numerous demolition bombs. The Aussies, too, left patches of fire and smoke in their wake.

American GIs on the line watched the air attacks with little enthusiasm. The 5th Air Force planes had attacked Japanese positions yesterday and the day before. But still the enemy jungle fighters had launched heavy attacks after dark to send the American GIs in retreat with heavy losses.

The U.S. dogfaces had guessed correctly. After the Allied aerial attacks, Japanese soldiers once more popped out of their sheltered holes. The air attacks had slain about 20 men and injured some 50 more around Anamo, while destroying about two tons of supplies. When Colonel Nara got reports from subordinates, he found that most of his Coastal Force was pretty much intact.

"We are still quite strong," Major Yamashita told the 237th Infantry commander. "If the enemy does not conduct more air strikes today, we can attack their ground troops again tonight to make more gains."

"I do not believe they will make new attacks," Nara said. "Anyway, we have taken excellent precautions."

At the battered village of Chinapelli, Colonel Ide viewed the flattened huts, charred trees, and tangles of fallen limbs. He then turned to a subordinate. "How badly have we suffered?"

"About a dozen men killed and perhaps thirty wounded," the captain said. "We also lost considerable supplies. However, if the Americans do not conduct further air attacks today, we can continue our offensive tonight."

Ide pursed his lips. "Perhaps the enemy feels they have done enough and will not return. What of Lt. Colonel Tsuji?"

"I regret to say, colonel, that his force has suffered badly from these new aerial strikes. Nearly one hundred of his men were killed or wounded, and he has lost much of his supplies."

"That is unfortunate," Ide said. "He may not be strong enough for a new assault tonight. Tell him to move away from the river bank, for the shoreline is obviously an easy target for these Yankee and Australian airmen."

"Yes, colonel," the subordinate said.

"Meanwhile, be sure the men remain on alert. There is always the possibility that the enemy will conduct more air strikes."

Along the southern sector, Colonel Matsumoto studied the burning village of Afua and the smoking forests to the west. Immediately after the air raids, he sent aides to evaluate damage and casualties. Now he spoke to them. "Well?"

"We only suffered minor casualties," the 1st Battalion commander said. "We have counted fifteen men killed and another twenty-two wounded. However, we lost considerable supplies, and I am not certain that our First Battalion will have enough provisions for a night time assault across the X-ray River."

"Such news is distressing." the 78th Regiment commander said. "Perhaps we will need to postpone any further attacks until more supplies reach us. I am told that pack animals are carrying such provisions over the jungle trails from Wewak, while barges are bringing in supplies up the coast."

"What shall I do?"

"Remain in your defenses," Matsumoto said. "Rest your men. Meanwhile, I will contact General Miyake for his counsel."

"Yes, colonel."

Of the three airstrikes conducted by the 3rd and 475th U.S. Groups during the past three days, these attacks on this July 12 morning had been the most damaging. The Japanese were now relatively exposed along the rivers, about the small jungle villages, and along the coastal area, as opposed to their previous positions in the remote, dense jungle brakes. General Miyake, however, still hoped to continue his offensive operations, and he urged the 18th Army staff in Wewak to hasten the movement of supplies to his forces west of the Driniumor River. Such units as Tsuji's 2nd Battalion, which had suffered considerable losses, were in desperate need of provisions. The Aitape Assault Force commander wanted enough stores by dark to continue his drive westward.

Naively, General Miyake did not anticipate further air attacks today. He expected the Americans to follow the same pattern that had cost U.S. ground forces a series of defeats on two successive nights. However, Gen. William Gill had certainly recognized the futility of the intermittent air strikes. He called 5th Air Force headquarters and insisted that strikes be conducted throughout the day. Then, Gill came up with a unique, secondary plan to stop the Japanese.

At 0900 hours, July 12, Gill met with his regimental commanders, Colonel Fowler of the 128th Infantry, Colonel Howe of the 127th Infantry, and Lt. Colonel Hooper of the 112th Cavalry Regiment. Also at the conference were Capt. William Dale of the 114th Combat Engineer Battalion and Maj. William Lewis of the U.S. 129th Field Artillery. Also here was Maj. Paul Becker of the 44th Tank Battalion.

"Gentlemen," Gill began, "if we don't stop the Nips they could take Aitape and the Tadji airdromes. The morale of our troops is at a low ebb and another defeat would finish them."

"They're like moles," Colonel Howe said. "Those Nips just dig themselves underground and stay there. Our attacks don't seem to hurt them much."

"That's because we haven't been hitting them hard enough," Gill gestured. "We won't make the same mistake today. I've asked Fifth Air Force to hit suspected enemy positions all day for the rest of the day. If that doesn't destroy them, such continual air strikes will keep them so deep in their holes they can't organize themselves for new attacks after dark. And," the 32nd Infantry commander grinned, "by this time tonight, we'll have the means to stop them in a ground attack."

The regimental commanders frowned, but the Red Arrow commander grinned again. He turned to William Dale. "Captain?"

The 114th Combat Engineer commander nodded and spread a map on the desk. "I'd like you to look at this," he said, running a finger over some blue penciled lines. "Here's the coastal road from Aitape: across the Nigia River, through Tiver, across the Koronal, through Anamo, and then on to the banks of the Driniumor. Down here in the center is the Kamti Trail that runs from Tadji Plantation to the Nigia River, then to the X-ray, through Chinapelli, and also to the Driniumor. And here in the south," Dale moved his fingers again, "is the Palauru Track running from Maiwi to the Nigia River, then westward across the X-ray, through Afua, and on to the Driniumor."

The regimental commanders only frowned and Dale continued. "North and south," he moved his finger again, "we have a decent trail running from Aitape village to Maiwi. We also have trails along the Nigia and Koronal Rivers and we have the Anamo Track along the Driniumor between Anamo and Afua."

222

"We're familiar with these tracks," Colonel Howe said, somewhat irritably. "What are you getting at?"

"As I understand, colonel, the major problem is a lack of heavy artillery to match those 75mm guns and 90mm mortar of the Japanese."

"That's true," Howe nodded. "I don't know how the hell they get those big weapons up here, but I'm told they dismantle them, carry them on pack horses, and then reassemble them."

"Well," Major Lewis suddenly spoke. "we think we can move our own big guns through the jungle as well as tanks."

Merle Howe squeezed his face, puzzled.

"Merle," General Gill said, "I was observing Captain Dale's engineering crews at Tadji. Their bulldozers were cutting a swath through the jungle for that new bomber strip. They opened a path over a mile long and one hundred yards wide in a few hours. I was amazed."

"Those D-eight dozers can plow through anything, general," Captain Dale grinned. He looked at Colonel Fowler. "I believe your forces are now at Tiver on the Koronal River, about two miles west of Anamo. And you, sir," he looked at Colonel Howe, "have your troops of the First Battalion along the Nigia River, a few miles west of Chinapelli."

The 127th Infantry commander nodded.

Then, the aviation engineer officer looked at Peter Cooper. "Colonel, your troops are on the X-ray in the vicinity of the Palauru Track, about

223

three miles west of Afua. Is that correct?"

"Yes," Hooper said.

"Suppose you had 205 and 155 artillery pieces in your positions?" Lewis asked. "Wouldn't that help you to push back those enemy troops?"

"My God," Hooper hissed, "we could pulverize them with 205s, especially if the artillery fire was coordinated with air attacks."

"Captain Dale, at my request, has suspended operations on the air strip," General Gill said. "He will use his bulldozers to widen these tracks eastward so we can move artillery pieces and tanks to the front lines. We'll use TDs to haul the guns behind the dozers and tanks can obviously drive themselves. We should have those big guns and armor up to your current positions by evening. If the Japanese try any new attacks tonight, they'll get a real shock. And," the general gestured, "as we push the enemy back, the dozers will continue eastward along the trails so we can move these guns and tanks after the enemy as soon as ground forces clear Japanese positions. Our objective is to restore the Driniumor River line and to destroy the enemy in the process."

The regimental colonels only listened.

"We'll be using a pair of dozers on each trail," Dale said, "two over the coastal trail in the north, two over the Kamti Trail in the center, and two over the Palauru Track in the south."

"Battery A of the One-twenty-ninth Field Artillery will bring six 155s and six 205s along the northern trail to support the One-twenty-eighth," Gill continued. "Battery B will bring up a dozen 205s and 105s in the center, and Battery C will move its twelve big guns along the Palauru Track. We'll also assign six Sherman tanks to each regiment. That armor and their 75mm guns should be of real help."

"Can we actually move those guns and armor through that thick jungle?" Colonel Fowler asked.

"Sir," the 129th Field Artillery commander said, "we've moved big guns through the jungle before, at Lae and Finchhaven, and we can do it again."

"We've had our Shermans growling through jungles at Saidor and Buna," Major Paul Becker suddenly spoke. "If those dozers give us an eight foot trail, my Forty-fourth Tank Battalion crews will move that armor, I guarantee it."

Fowler grinned at Captain Dale. "If you get those big guns and armor up to us for close support, I promise—we'll push those Nips back across the Driniumor."

"We've got the entire Sixteenth TD Battalion with over forty treaded vehicles to haul those guns," Major Lewis said. "We'll have that artillery and those tanks up to your positions within the next twelve hours."

"Fine," Colonel Howe nodded.

"Okay," General Gill sighed, "get back to your units."

By 1000 hours, a half dozen D-8 bulldozers were growling over the jungle trails, felling trees in their path, swathing away limbs, flattening dense brush, and opening an eight foot wide jungle road. Meanwhile, Major Lewis had hooked up artillery caissons to TDs and the treaded vehicles easily towed the guns over the newly hewn jungle roads behind the dozers. Behind the gun caissons came the rumbling 33 ton medium tanks and their short barreled 75mm guns that were ideal for close in-fighting. The dozers made nearly 350 yards an hour and they expected to reach the most forward American positions by 2100.

Even as the bulldozers of the 114th Engineers cut roads through the jungle, 5th Air Force launched more attacks against Japanese positions. At 1020 hours, 40 Havocs of the 312th Bomb Group, also out of Hollandia, escorted by P-38s of Maj. Harry Brown's 9th Squadron, worked over the Japanese positions in the Anamo area with 100 pound demolition bombs and raking .50 caliber nose gun fire. Moments later, the RAAF Beauforts out of Tadji swept over the Afua area with bombing and strafing attacks. By noon of July 12, the 3rd and 475th Groups had returned to the Aitape area for their second strike of the day.

Before General Miyake and his Aitape Assault Force troops could recover from these 5th Air Force morning attacks, the 312th Bomb Group, the 9th Fighter Squadron, and the 90 Wing were back again at 1400 hours with more whistling bombs, chattering machine gun fire, and descending parafrags. Then, at 1600, the 3rd Bomb Group and 475th Fighter Group came to Aitape for their third strike of the day. And finally, just before dark, at about 1800 hours, airmen of the 312th Group and the 40 Wing roared over the suspected Japanese positions with another low level bombing and strafing attack.

Explosions, fires, and smoke now prevailed in the jungle between the Driniumor and forward American positions. Not until 2000 hours, well into the evening, did the Japanese finally win a respite. For more than two hours, they snuffed out fires, cleared away debris, tended wounded, buried dead, and salvaged supplies. At 2200 hours, General Miyake met with his commanders.

"This has been a devastating day. The Americans have reverted to their old tricks of bombing and strafing our positions without let up during daylight hours. Our troops have not enjoyed a moment's rest all day. I regret to say that there has been extensive damage around my own headquarters, and we have suffered death and injury to our headquarters company. I can assume that other units have suffered similiar damage and casualties."

Colonel Ide pursed his lips before he spoke. "I must tell you that the Afua positions are in ruins and that the First Battalion is still counting its losses in men and supplies."

Miyake nodded and looked at Colonel Nara: "What of your Coastal Force?"

"We abandoned Anamo at midday, after the third enemy strike," Nara said, "for the village and the open areas surrounding the coastal town became quite untenable. However, most of my force is still able and they are resting in the jungles south and east of Anamo."

"Good," Miyake said. "And what of your Eightieth Regiment?" he looked at Colonel Ide.

"Lt. Colonel Tsuji's battalion has suffered terrible losses. Fortunately, he moved his troops east of the river after the first attack this morning, so he has not suffered as badly as he might have. As for the remainder of my regiment, we have counted about one hundred dead and wounded."

"I realize the severe physical and mental anguish these multiple enemy air strikes have caused your forces," Miyake said. "Still, I propose that we conduct another offensive tonight."

"Honorable Miyake," Colonel Ide gasped, "surely you cannot be serious. Our troops have been seriously hurt. They need rest to recompose themselves."

"That is exactly what the enemy expects," Miyake said. "The Americans must surely suspect that their bombers have left us badly decimated and that we cannot continue our offensive. I believe we could catch the Americans

228

completely off guard."

The officers did not answer.

"Despite the enemy air strikes, more supplies have come across the Driniumor River, and service troops will deliver them to the Eightieth and Seventy-eighth Regiment positions by midnight." He looked at Nara. "Three barges even now approach the shoreline east of Anamo. They carry more than five hundred tons of ammunition, food, and other supplies for your Coastal Force. The provisions should reach you within an hour."

Nara only stared soberly at the Aitape Assault Force commander.

"I see a serious doubt in your faces," Miyake said, "but I insist that the opportunity will never be better than it can be on this night." He pulled a sheet of paper from his pocket. "The Honorable Adachi himself will arrive here by morning. What better gift can we offer him than news of another victory?"

"Perhaps you are right," Colonel Matsumoto wavered. "My troops will do whatever is asked of them. I can assure you, they will charge across the X-ray River if we ask them to do so."

"I know that Lt. Colonel Tsuji will not hesitate," Colonel Ide said, "even if he must charge over the Nigia River with one hundred men."

"If the Honorable Matsumoto and the Honorable Ide are willing to mount new attacks after our suffering today," Colonel Nara said, "then we of the Coastal Force must be equally willing. I can muster my troops at once to cross the Koronal River and drive the Americans from Tiver."

"Good," Miyake nodded. "We shall begin the usual artillery and mortar barrages ten or fifteen minutes before midnight. Then, your troops may attack. I am certain we will succeed tonight as we did last night and the night before."

Thus, however battered from the series of 5th Air Force strikes, the Japanese prepared for new assaults.

But conditions would change radically before the midnight witching hour. At 2000 hours, at Tiver on the west bank of the Koronal River, Sgt. Henry Cooper and Cpl. Joe Cartwright stood on alert. But, they turned in astonishment as growling bulldozers, toppling trees and crushing brush before them, clattered into the Koronel River bank positions of the 128th Regiment.

"Good Christ," Cartwright huffed, "what the hell are those dozers doin' here?"

"Beats the hell out of me," Cooper answered.

But a moment later, the two non-coms from G Company showed even more surprise when they heard the rumbling TDs hauling 155mm and 205mm artillery caissons over the widened trail. Before the GIs absorbed this astonishing sight, they heard and then saw the rumbling Sherman tanks. The bulldozers quickly cleared a wide patch of ground along the Koronal River before TDs hauled the 12 big caissons into position along the banks.

"Son of a bitch," Corporal Cartwright gasped.

"Jesus," Sergeant Cooper huffed, "if those Nips try to overrun us tonight, they'll get chopped to pieces."

"You know," Cartwright grinned, "I almost wish they'd try a banzai charge across the river. I'd like to see the faces of those mother fuckers when they get hit by those big guns and those Sherman tanks."

"Yes sir," Cooper nodded, "if they come again tonight, they'll be in for a real shock."

In the center positions along the Nigia River, Col. Merle Howe and his 1st Battalion CO, Lt. Col. Ed Basler, jerked from an early evening respite when they heard the bulldozers growling forward from the depths of the forests. Howe knew they were coming, but he was surprised to see them here so soon. Basler and the others, however, gaped in astonishment at the strange sight. As the D-8s appeared on the river bank, Capt. William Dale himself stood upright next to the dozer driver.

"Where do you want these guns, colonel?" the captain grinned.

"Spread them along the river for about five hundred yards," Howe said, "and intersperse the tanks. Can your dozers do that?"

"You got it, colonel," Dale said before he

gestured to his driver.

By 2200 hours, 12 big American artillery pieces had been stationed along the river bank, with a half dozen Sherman tanks in between, the armor aiming their 75mm barrels toward the dark depths of the jungle on the opposite bank. If Tsuji's 2nd Battalion charged across the Nigia, he would charge into oblivion.

At 2300 hours, on the X-ray River to the south, Sgt. Ed Madcliff had been checking defense positions with Captain Lowry when they heard the growl of heavy vehicles in the dark brakes behind them. The two men frowned and then Lowry's eyes widened when he saw the big dozer lumbering toward him, the huge blade scraping and smashing dense brush in its path.

"For Christ sake," Lowry hissed, "what the hell's going on?"

"Goddamn if I know, captain," Sergeant Madcliff shook his head.

"What the hell are those dozers doing here?"

The sergeant only shrugged.

Then the two men from I Company ogled at the sight behind the bulldozers—TDs dragging artillery caissons and six Sherman tanks taking up the rear. The two men turned when Lt. Colonel Hooper approached them with a grin.

"Big guns and M-four tanks," the 112th Cavalry commander said, "They've brought in a dozen 205s and 155s. Those dozers have been hacking through the jungle all day. If the Nips try to hit us tonight, they'll get a real hot reception."

"Twelve field pieces and six tanks?" Lowry asked in disbelief.

Hooper nodded. The lt. colonel then ordered the guns and tanks spread out on a 500 yard front behind the banks of the X-ray River. By 2230 hours, the surprised but elated GIs had unloaded dozens of artillery shells from ammo carriers and stacked the explosives in neat piles near the big guns. Madcliff directed one of the work parties and when he finished the gun chief grinned.

"Thanks, sarge," the Battery C artilleryman said. "If those Nips try any banzai charge tonight, they'll get torn to pieces."

"I believe you," Madcliff nodded.

By 2330 hours, the Americans had entrenched themselves in position: at Tiver to the north, the Nigia River in the center, and on the X-ray River to the south. Gunners of the 129th's A, B, and C Batteries stood by their cannons, while tank crews of the 44th Tank Battalion waited inside their M-4s. Every GI peered into the dark, shadowy trees to the east. As usual, the brakes looked quiet and deserted, but the Americans suspected that Japanese jungle fighters were there, and that they would try banzai charges tonight as they had during the past two nights.

At 2345 hours, the Japanese confirmed the suspicions of the GIs. Rattling Japanese 75mm fire and 90mm mortar fire suddenly erupted into the American positions: at Tiver village, along the Nigia River, and east of the X-ray River.

American soldiers cowered in their foxholes and trenches, waiting for the assault that would follow the barrage. They knew the Japanese would pour westward as soon as the cannonades lifted, and the GIs cursed. Again! The Japanese had again chosen the midnight witching hour to assail the Americans.

But at 2350 hours, the GIs of the Red Arrow Infantry Division heard something they had not heard on the two previous nights.

"Fire! Open fire!" The same cry echoed from artillery and tank commanders at Tiver, at the Nigia, and at the X-ray.

Then, the jungle shook and vibrated from numbing shells that barked from the river banks. The staccato of blasts almost deafened the cowering GIs as whistling 205, 155, and 75 shells spewed eastward into the Japanese forces from the American artillery and tanks. The exploding balls of fire were so loud and bright, they almost blinded the GIs of the 32nd Division. Not one tree, but several trees at a time toppled in loud thuds, while huge limbs by the scores crashed to the jungle earth. The heavy American barrages echoed throughout the length of the jungle, from the coastal town of Tiver all the way south to the foot of the Toricelli Mountains.

At Tiver, Sgt. Henry Cooper stood upright in his trench, utterly exposed, and stared at the huge, bursting orange flashes in the jungles across the Koronal River. "Jesus Christ, will you look at that! Look at that!"

Next to Cooper, Cpl. Joe Cartwright stared with the same awe. "Hank, nobody can survive that stuff over there; nobody at all."

"Yeh," Sgt. Henry Cooper nodded.

Chapter Thirteen

In the defenses around Anamo, Col. Masahuko Nara was stunned by the heavy 205 and 105 cannon fire, along with the 75mm tank shells. The numbing explosions had killed and maimed dozens of his troops. Even the deeply dug, log covered foxholes could not shelter the Coastal Force soldiers. Widespread explosions destroyed them in clumps and mere concussions from the 205mm eruptions killed hordes of Japanese infantrymen. Further, the booming, heavy cannonade had mangled many of the 75mm guns and 90mm mortar tubes. By 2355 hours, a mere five minutes after the U.S. barrage began, the 129th U.S. Field Artillery gunners and the 44th Tank Battalion crews had ripped apart the Japanese positions.

Above the din of heavy fire, Maj. Tadi Yamashita wove through the explosions to find Nara. "Colonel, we are suffering severe casualties. We must retreat; we must retreat."

Nara stared dumbfoundedly at the huge,

blinding flashes that burst amidst his jungle complement of troops. He himself occasionally cringed from a shattering reverberation, a toppling tree trunk, or a falling limb. "We must respond," the Coastal Force commander cried.

"It is impossible, colonel, impossible," Yamashita shook his head. "Our entire regiment will be destroyed if we remain here. There is no possibility of making an assault into Tiver through such heavy cannon fire. We would lose every man in our unit."

"How did they get these big guns to the Koronal River?" Nara screamed. "How did they do so?"

"I do not know," Yamashita said, "but I beg you—we must retreat before we are all slain. We do not know how many shells the enemy has, but I would not be surprised if they continued this heavy cannonade throughout the night."

"Very well," Nara nodded before he cringed from another erupting ball of fire. "We will retire south over the Anamo Trail to our old positions on the banks of the Driniumor River."

"Yes, colonel," Yamashita answered. The major then wove again through the heavy artillery fire to find the various company commanders and direct a retreat. He had just issued orders to Captain Sugino, Lieutenant Onizuka, and a few others when a whistling shell exploded squarely in front of the 1st Battalion commander. Against the brightness of the orange burst, a pair of jungle fighters saw the major's

237

body fly upwards like a bouncing, silhouetted figure. A moment later they found Yamashita's riddled body, grotesque and bloody, lying on the jungle floor in a distorted heap.

Meanwhile, Captain Sugino, Lieutenant Onizuka, and other 237th Regiment officers quickly directed their men out of the area and took them southward, out of range from the heavy 205mm and 155mm fire. Non coms like Sgt. Kiyoshi Itoh maintained excellent discipline in the face of heavy fire and their calmness mitigated the panic that had gripped the Japanese soldiers.

"Move swiftly, swiftly," Itoh gestured to his platoon. "We must escape the area to avoid further death and injury."

Lieutenant Onizuka also did a good job of stopping a haphazard stampede. While he directed troops southeast, away from the Anamo sector and toward the Driniumor River, he cautioned his troops. "Remain in single file, but move quickly. Do not hesitate and slow up those behind you. If anyone is killed or injured from the enemy barrage, you will move over or around him and leave the wounded men to medical attendants."

By 0130 hours, when the American barrage lifted, survivors of the Coastal Force had already moved quite far to the southeast. An eerie silence then prevailed in the battered brakes on the opposite side of the Koronal River. Wisps of smoke rose from the area and bright fires flickered within the rain forests beyond Anamo. Capt. Tally Fulmer of the American G Company walked to the river bank and peered to the east through field glasses. He saw nothing in the minced brakes: no movements, no enemy soldiers, nothing.

"What do you think, sir?" Sgt. Henry Cooper asked.

"I think they've run off; retreated down the trail."

"Can you be certain, captain?"

Fulmer nodded. "I'm sure they planned to attack around midnight, but they never came. No, this heavy shelling chopped them to pieces."

"What do we do now, sir?" Cooper asked.

"I don't know," the captain said. "I'll check with battalion. Where's my radio man?"

"Right here, sir."

Fulmer nodded and called Lt. Col. Henry Geebs. "Colonel, the Nips have apparently abandoned their positions on the other side of the river. There's enough fires there to light up the brakes like a Coney Island midway. We don't see a sign of life. What do you think? What do you want us to do?"

"Not a goddamn thing," Geebs answered. "Regiments says to stay put. Just dig into your positions for the rest of the night and we'll cross the river in the morning. We'll probably follow those Nips at first light."

"Yes sir," Captain Fulmer said.

The GIs of G Company along with other

239

dogfaces of the 128th Regiment felt an invigorating relief. There would be no banzai charges against their defenses. They stared at the big barrels of the 155mm and 205mm guns, as well as the medium Sherman tanks. The U.S. soldiers were grateful to the engineers who had opened a path for these weapons and they appreciated the cannoneers who had accurately pulverized the enemy troops on the other side of the Koronal River.

In the south, the indomitable Sgt. Ed Madcliff of the Lowry Force had agreed to reconnoiter the terrain east of the X-ray River beyond the defenses of the 112th Cavalry and the two companies of the 127th Regiment under Capt. Leonard Lowry. Madcliff and his small squad of scouts had conducted their usual stealthy, undetected job of studying the enemy's deployment. The American patrol came as close as 20 yards to the forward Japanese troops of the 78th Regiment which was about ½ mile east of the river.

"What do you think, sarge?" one of the scouts whispered to Madcliff.

"I think there must be a thousand of the bastards in there," the non-com answered in the same low voice. "We'll get a line on their depth."

For another half hour, Madcliff and his scouts moved quietly through the dense, dark jungle to the east and south laterals of the Japanese positions. They then probed eastward to get a more exact picture of the Japanese complement. The sergeant, with the uncanny visual ability of a cat in the dark, carefully noted the Japanese positions. The scrutiny confirmed his suspicions—perhaps an entire regiment, although understrength, lay in the patch of jungle. Madcliff also made mental notes on the approximate number of mortars and 75mm guns the enemy had. No doubt, the Japanese jungle fighters were preparing to move out: strapping on ammo belts, donning helmets, and checking weapons. The enemy obviously intended to conduct new attacks this evening across the X-ray River and into the American positions.

Finally, at 2130 hours, the patrol leader motioned to his squad. "Okay we've seen enough."

About an hour later, Madcliff and his men had reached the American positions on the west side of the X-ray. He met immediately with Captain Lowry and Lt. Colonel Hooper. "They intend to attack soon," Madcliff said. "I'd guess they'll storm across the river at their usual time, sir; around midnight."

"How can you be that certain, sergeant?" Hooper asked with a hint of doubt.

"Colonel, sir, they'll attack at midnight, I guarantee it," Madcliff answered sharply.

"The sergeant knows what he's talking about, colonel," Captain Lowry told Hooper. "Madcliff is one of the best scouts in our division. He was the man who brought us the verified information that the Japanese were moving west from Wewak to attack Aitape in force. I'd stake my life on anything Madcliff told me."

"You've got that much faith in him?" Hooper grinned.

"Yes sir," Lowry nodded vigorously.

"Okay," the 112th Cavalry commander nodded. "We've got those artillery guns and tanks up here now and we've got our troops well dug in. We'll alert them to be ready for a possible enemy attack around midnight."

"Why should we wait, sir?" Madcliff said. "Why not hit them now, before they launch any attack? We can give those artillerymen good coordinates to zero in on their location. We know exactly where those Nips are mustering."

"Exactly?"

"Yes sir."

Lt. Col. Peter Hooper grinned again. "As I said, I'll take Captain Lowry's word on your ability and judgment." He then ordered the Battery C commander and the tank unit commander to aim their 155, 205, and 75mm guns on the enemy positions as designated by Sergeant Madcliff. "I want a rolling barrage over the entire area," Hooper said. "As soon as you finish one sweep, start over."

"How long shall we keep up the shelling?" the artillery officer asked.

"Until I tell you to stop."

"Yes sir."

At 2300 hours, Colonel Matsumoto was still

preparing his men, 75mm cannon, and 90mm mortar for the attack on the Americans on the X-ray River. He felt relatively safe. But then suddenly, the American Battery C opened with a cannonade of bursting shells that shattered the dead silence. Concussioning orange balls soon brightened the jungle darkness as 205mm and 155mm hits exploded in numbing blasts squarely on the Japanese 78th Regiment positions. A moment later, 75mm shells from the Sherman tanks also laced the enemy positions.

From the river bank, with the aid of light from the blinding flashes, GIs saw the small dark figures scampering about wildly in the depths of the jungle to escape the heavy U.S. cannonade. Dozens of black shapes, Japanese soldiers, flew skyward in erupting balls of fire. The Americans even heard the agonizing screams that pierced the din of thumping tree trunks and cracking limbs.

"Goddamn it, colonel," Lowry said, "we're right on the button."

"We've got them zeroed in perfectly," Hooper answered. He then looked at Madcliff and grinned. "Sergeant, remind me to put you and your scouts in for Silver Stars."

"Thank you, sir."

In the 78th Regiment positions, Col. Mitsujiro Matsumoto stood rigid, utterly stupefied by the pinpoint accuracy of the American cannon fire. He had stiffened into a near comatose state from the shelling that was now slaughtering his troops. He made no attempt to even shelter himself as he looked in horror at the hordes of dead that fell about him or the scores of injured who flopped about the potted jungle floor like wounded snakes. Nor did he react to the agonizing screams and moans of these dying and wounded men.

"Colonel, we must retreat, we must retreat," the 1st Battalion major cried. "You must authorize a retreat."

Matsumoto looked at his subordinate but only blinked.

"Please, colonel, I implore you. Please authorize a retreat!"

"Yes, yes," the 78th Regiment commander finally nodded, shaking himself from his near trance. "We will retire to Afua on the Driniumor River. You will so instruct the company commanders."

"Thank you, colonel."

Moments later, the Japanese, those still able, withdrew hastily eastward, away from the numbing blasts that had brought death and destruction to so many of their comrades. The 1st Battalion commander all but assumed command of the retreat for Matsumoto himself was still in a near state of shock.

Within 15 minutes after the American barrage began, the Japanese had totally abandoned their positions east of the X-ray River. They now staggered through the jungle, moving frantically. The 78th Regiment infantrymen were numb with fear. Their bodies trembled, and perspiration dampened them from head to foot. The Nippon jungle fighters now sought only one goal—escape from the concussioning American shells.

At 2330 hours, Lt. Colonel Hooper called off the barrage. "By now, they're either dead or they've run off."

"Are we going after them, sir?" Captain Lowry asked.

"Not tonight; we'll cross the river in the morning."

"Do you want Madcliff to take another look?"

The lt. colonel looked at the non-com and grinned. "The sergeant did one hell of a job, but first light tomorrow will be soon enough to take a look."

Five miles to the northwest, on the west bank of the Nigia River, Col. Merle Howe and Capt. Herman Botcher of E Company had just completed rounds among the E and H Company ranks. Maj. William Lewis, meanwhile, had completed checking his 129th Artillery cannoneers. Then, the three officers sat down for late evening coffee in Colonel Howe's tent.

"We're ready," Lewis said, "and the tank crews are ready."

"We've got to throw them back," Howe said. "If they break through us, nothing will stop them from overrunning the Tadji airdromes."

"We'll stop them," Lewis promised. "I don't

care how many of those Nips try to cross the river, they won't make it through those big shells; and they sure as hell won't get by those Sherman tanks."

Captain Botcher looked at Howe. "Colonel, the flyboys have been plastering those Nips all day. I don't know how they can mount another offensive tonight."

"If they only have a hundred able men, they'll try to hit us," Howe said.

"It's too bad we don't know the enemy's exact positions across the river," Major Lewis said. "We could start hitting them right now."

"Just aim your guns on the river, Major," Howe said.

Across the X-ray River, Lt. Col. Masanasubo Tsuji took stock. He had suffered over 200 dead and wounded since the battles began on the night of July 10-11, and he could only muster about 400 men for a new assault. But, Tsuji was determined to reach the Tadji airdromes. He had come too far and suffered too much to lose the prize now. After making rounds, he visited the 80th Regiment commander.

"Colonel, I would like to start across the river at once."

"Our attack is scheduled for midnight," Ide answered.

"That is what the Americans expect of us," Tsuji said. "If we strike now, we may surprise them and more easily overrun them."

Colonel Ide pursed his lips. "Are your troops ready?"

"They have been waiting for a new attack since dusk."

"How many of your soldiers are able to make an assault?"

"About four hundred," the 2nd Battalion commander said. "Captain Kitazona has charged his men and Sergeant Toga assures me that the enemy is complacent at this hour."

"Very well," Ide nodded, "you will launch an assault in a half hour. That will give me time to ready the Third Battalion whose troops will follow your own battalion."

Thus on July 12, an hour ahead of schedule, Lt. Colonel Tsuji mustered his depleted battalion in three ranks to make successive charges across the Nigia River. At 2300 hours, the first body of Japanese jungle fighters burst out of the dark trees and waded into the river with upraised weapons.

"Banzai! Banzai!" The cries stiffened the GIs on the opposite bank.

But the Americans were ready. Unfortunately for the Japanese, Maj. William Lewis had already moved among the artillerymen and tank crews to begin a barrage into the suspected Japanese positions east of the Nigia River. Lt. Colonel Tsuji's troops had thus splashed into the Nigia River at exactly the wrong moment. As the gray clad shapes hit the water, Major Lewis gave the shouting order:

"Fire! Open fire!"

Seconds later, the jungle shook as a dozen

155mm and 205mm cannon, along with six 75mm tank guns, fired almost from point blank range. The U.S. gunners sent screaming shells into the rushing Japanese soldiers. Exploding bursts of fire shredded the 80th Infantry troops in geysers of spraying shrapnel. Hordes of men disappeared in numbing blasts or plopped into the slow moving stream; or they died from crashing limbs and falling trees before they even reached the river bank. The heavy barrage cut the enemy ranks to pieces before they had come halfway across the Nigia.

American GIs shuddered from the deafening blasts that erupted only 100 to 150 yards away from their positions. They opened their mouths to temper the din and avoid possible deafness.

For nearly ten minutes, the heavy artillery fire cut down rows of Tsuji's troops and finally, the lt. colonel ordered a retreat. However, by the time he mustered survivors, he found only about 100 able men left in his battalion. Hundreds of Japanese troops lay in mangled heaps along the river bank, half buried under debris, or floating atop the surface of the Nigia River. Among the missing were Sergeant Toga and Captain Kitazona. Tsuji himself was utterly shocked by the artillery assault and he called Colonel Ide.

"They have heavy cannon. We cannot possibly breach their defenses. I fear that most of my troops have been slain."

"We must consider what to do next," Ide said.

However, before the 80th Regiment commander could digest this bad news from his 2nd Battalion commander, Maj. William Lewis unleashed a rolling barrage into the darkened jungle positions. Soon, other troops in Ide's command suffered death and injury from the numbing artillery blasts. Ide saw no choice but to retreat.

"We will retire to the Driniumor River."

"I agree," a discouraged Lt. Colonel Tsuji answered.

Colonel Ide was soon directing Japanese soldiers swiftly to the eastward. He did not stop at the smashed villages of Chinapelli or Palauru as he drove his men toward the Driniumor. But, Major Lewis had adjusted range and heavy artillery followed the retreating 80th Regiment troops along the Kamti Trail. The cannon fire killed and maimed more of the Japanese during the anxious retreat. Not until after midnight did Lewis finally lift the barrage.

In the renewed silence, Colonel Howe peered at the palls of smoke across the river and the dozens of fires that still raged in the area. In the light of the flames, the 127th Regiment commander saw clearly the countless Japanese dead.

"What do we do now, colonel?" Captain Botcher asked.

"Cross the river in the morning."

"I think the bulldozers ought to be on the other side first," Major Lewis said. "If you're going to follow those retreating Japanese, you'll want our heavy artillery to keep hitting them in the ass.''

"That's for sure, Major," Howe nodded with a grin.

At first light, July 13, the squealing lorie birds and squawking mynah birds woke most of the GIs of the Red Arrow 32nd Infantry before sergeants rousted them from their abbreviated sleep. After a simple K ration breakfast, all three regiments moved out: the 128th across the Koronal River into Anamo, the 127th troops across the Nigia River and into Chinapelli, and the Lowry Force with the 112th troopers across the X-ray toward Afua.

American GIs stared aghast at the sights along the eastward treks: hundreds of dead Japanese lay in heaps, scattered along the jungle trails, torn to ribbons in deep craters, or half buried under debris. The GIs also found battered and abandoned 75mm guns, 90mm mortar tubes, mounds of burned out supplies, and slain pack animals. As the Americans plodded forward, they frequently moved aside to accommodate the growling bulldozers that once more widened the paths eastward. Immediately behind the D-8s, TDs rumbled again with trailing artillery caissons, and behind them the Sherman tanks. And finally, ammo carriers followed in the rear of the strange vehicular caravans.

Meanwhile, the sudden change of fortunes had prompted the Japanese to assault the trapped U.S. C Company under Capt. George Royce. The Nippon soldiers, in apparent frustration, charged into the C Company positions at dawn. The Americans fired furiously into the charging platoons of gray clad men, downing more than a dozen of them before the enemy retreated. However, Captain Royce was not certain he could hold off another charge.

"How much ammo do we have, sergeant?" Royce asked Gerry Endl.

"Maybe enough for another ten minute skirmish."

Royce squeezed his face. "If they come again, make every shot count."

"Yes sir."

Moments later, the numbing cry erupted once more. "Banzai! Banzai!" Then, the screaming hordes again charged the American positions. The GIs fired furiously, but they could not hold. "Retreat! Retreat!" Royce cried.

The Americans left their defenses and scattered south into the jungle, with Sgt. Gerry Endl firing a hand held .50 caliber machine gun at the Japanese to open a path. Nearly a dozen Americans fell wounded from return fire and Endl then made quick shuttling runs to drag the wounded out before the Japanese occupied the hastily vacated C Company positions. The sergeant had brought out an astonishing eight wounded GIs. But then, as he went after a ninth man, Gerry L. Endl caught ripping machine gun fire that killed him and his burden. Still most of the GIs escaped the trap.

For his efforts, Endl won a posthumous Congressional Medal of Honor.

Before the Japanese could pursue the C Company GIs, the Japanese were joined by the retiring Coastal Force troops and they accompanied this unit in the retreat to the Driniumor, since Americans might be close on their heels. And in fact, by noon of July 13, pursuing GIs of the 128th Infantry caught up to the tattered C Company on the Anamo Trail.

"Goddamn, are we glad to see you," Royce grinned at Colonel Fowler.

The 128th Regiment commander nodded. "How bad were your casualties?"

"About twenty dead and wounded." Then, Royce frowned. "I lost Sergeant Endl. He brought out seven or eight wounded before he was killed himself."

"Too bad," Fowler said. Then he sighed. "Take your men back to the Tiver. You've suffered enough."

"Yes sir."

Meanwhile, 5th Air Force planes had been out since dawn, sending squadrons of planes to bomb and strafe the retiring Japanese at two hour intervals. Steady strafing fire, 100 pound demolition bombs, and descending parafrag bombs, wounded and killed dozens of the retreating 18th Army troops, leaving survivors spent and demoralized. Gen. Hatazo Adachi, who had crossed Driniumor River during mid-morning, met the first retreating Japanese by early afternoon. He listened in horror to the tales of agony and death suffered by his troops from the heavy artillery barrages and constant air attacks.

After Adachi took count of his casualties, he moaned in despair. His 18th Army had suffered 50 percent losses in dead and wounded. He had lost all of his 75mm guns and 90mm mortars. His troops were without food or other supplies. They had little ammunition for their rifles, and many of the wounded would die for lack of medicine.

"Honorable Adachi," General Miyake said, "we have no choice but to call off the offensive."

"That would be a shame after we have come so far."

"The Americans have excellent scouts," Miyake said. "I believe they knew our positions and perhaps they even suspect our poor condition. We can expect their air force to continue their attacks on us for the rest of the day, as they have been attacking us all morning. If we remain here, we will only suffer further casualties."

"Perhaps you are right," the 18th Army commander sighed. "We will rest our troops and then cross the Driniumor River in the morning."

But the Japanese would not enjoy the luxury of a night time respite. By dark, the bulldozers of the 114th U.S. Engineers had approached the old Driniumor River entrenchments from three directions, with artillery and tanks right behind them. Further, American patrols had deftly reconnoitered ahead to pinpoint the Japanese positions and all reports were essentially the same: the enemy was exhausted and without supplies, little ammunition, and no cannon. They were now congested along the Driniumor south of Anamo and north of Afua.

Gen. William Gill studied the reports eagerly and he then ordered a three prong artillery barrage. "I don't want them to dig in along the Driniumor or to have a minute's rest. I want the Japanese Eighteenth Army annihilated."

By 2100 hours, Maj. William Lewis had again brought his big guns into position and he opened fire.

A staccato of deafening blasts erupted from three directions, on the south from Afua, the center from Chinapelli, and the north from Anamo. Bursting shells slammed into the jammed 18th Army positions to elicit screams and moans from more dying and wounded Japanese soldiers. The Nippon troops raced about the patch of jungle in panic, trying desperately to avoid the nightmare of exploding shells in the dark, eerie tropical rain forests. The Japanese had not expected a renewed artillery assault this far east, and the 18th Army soldiers had not dug in for the night.

Within a few minutes more than 200 Nippon troops had been killed or wounded.

"We cannot remain here, Honorable Adachi,

254

we cannot stay," General Miyake said desperately.

"Retire the men across the river at once," Adachi said.

The Japanese soldiers, though battered and spent, moved quickly. They splashed across the Driniumor and scrambled up the east bank. However, the American artillerymen had anticipated such a retreat and they adjusted range to pummel the enemy as they melted to the east. More Japanese soldiers died before the remnants of the smashed Aitape Assault Force disappeared into the depths of the jungle.

By dawn of July 14, American troops moved warily into the old Driniumor River defenses. But caution had been unnecessary. The dogfaces found only countless dead on the narrow trails, within the jungle brush, atop the Driniumor's surface, or along the banks of the river.

"I guess we finished them," Captain Botcher told Colonel Howe.

The 127th commander nodded. "It's all over. They're finished. We've restored the Driniumor River line."

General Gill now reported to General Krueger, CinC of the U.S. 6th Army that the Japanese threat to Aitape was over. The decimated survivors of the 18th Army were fleeing eastward to Wewak. The Jungle Lizards of the U.S. 32nd Infantry Division had again mauled the 18th Army as the Red Arrows had mauled them at Buna, Finchhaven, and Saidor.

General Krueger soon relieved the Jungle Lizards and replaced them with the 124th and 169th Regiments, designated TED Force, under Gen. Julian Cunningham. On August 1, Cunningham marched his troops eastward across the Driniumor River as far as Yakamul without running into anything more than rear guard Japanese patrols. Only once, on August 5, did the Japanese attempt to stop the Americans. They sent a 400 man unit to attack TED Force at Yakamul. But, the GIs threw back the enemy, inflicting heavy losses while losing only two Americans.

As TED Force continued eastward, they killed more than 1,800 Japanese troops to a loss of 50 GIs killed and 80 wounded. Further, the U.S. 5th Air Force continued to attack the Japanese along the trails to Wewak.

On August 11, 1944, Gen. Walter Krueger sent a message to Cunningham: "TED Force may cease further pursuit of the enemy and return to the Driniumor River Line. The Japanese have been thoroughly defeated."

On August 25, Krueger declared the Aitape campaign officially over. The Americans had lost 440 men killed, 2,550 wounded, ten missing, and 2,000 GIs down with dengue, malaria, skin problems, and other disease. About a hundred American soldiers died from these diseases. Thus, the cost of the campaign had been high for the U.S. Persecution Force.

For the Japanese, however, the Aitape fight

had been a near disaster. Of the 2 1/3 divisions of troops committed to the campaign to recapture Aitape, Adachi had lost 8,821 killed and 90 captured. 2,000 more had been killed during the long retreat back to Wewak. Another 2,000 had suffered death from disease and starvation.

The battle had thus been one of the most vicious jungle struggles of the Pacific War.

The Japanese remained trapped in Wewak for another nine months, withering away from starvation in their trapped jungle bases. The Australians finally captured Wewak in May of 1945, although Adachi had escaped to the hills. The 18th Army commander did not surrender until September 10. The Australians later tried the Japanese general as a war criminal, condemned him, and sentenced him to life imprisonment. However, during the night of September 8-9, 1947, while in prison at Rabaul, Gen. Hatazo Adachi had somehow obtained a dagger in his cell and he committed suicide.

General William Gill said after the war: "I do not believe that General Adachi was a war criminal. He was merely a hard and determined fighter who almost drove us out of Aitape with much more inferior forces in numbers, arms, and equipment. He might have carried out this impossible feat except for the courage of our 32nd Infantry Division GIs, and perhaps the heavy artillery and Sherman tanks that we moved into the jungle front lines."

Bibliography

Books:

Alcorn, John, *The Jolly Rogers,* Historical
Aviation Album Publishers, Temple City,
Calif., 1981

Bjerre, Jens, *Savage New Guinea,* Tower Publi-
cations, New York City, 1964

Casey, Hugh T. General, *Engineers of the Southwest Pacific,* Office of Military History,
Washington, DC 1946

Craven, W.F., and Cate, J.L., *The Pacific:
Guadalcanal to Saipan,* Univ. of Chicago
Press, Chicago, 1964

Dexter, David, *The New Guinea Offensive,*
Australian War Memorial, Canberra, Australia, 1961

Eichelberger, Robert and Mackaye, Milton, *Our
Jungle Road to Tokyo,* Viking Press,
New York City, 1950

Forsberg Frank, edited by, *Yank—The GI Story
of the War,* Duell, Sloan, and Pearch Publishers, New York City, 1947

Greenfield, Kent Roberts, *War Against Japan,*
Office of Military History, U.S. Army, Washington, DC 1975

Jablonski, Edward, *Air War, Volume II,*
Doubleday & Co., Garden City, N.Y. 1971

Kenney, George C. General, *General Kenney
Reports: a Personal History of the Pacific
War,* Duell, Sloan & Pearce Publishers, New
York City, 1949

Marshall, G.C. General, chief of staff, *The
Aitape Campaign, 27 April-24 Aug 1944,*
Armed Forces in Action Series, Military Intelligence Division, War Department, Washington, DC, 1945

Morison, Samuel, *New Guinea and the
Marianas,* Little Brown & Co., Boston, 1953

Smith, Robert Ross, *Approach to the Philippines,* Office of Military History, U.S. Army,
Washington, DC, 1953

Steinberg, Rafael, *Island Fighting, World War
II,* Life Books Inc., Alexandria, Va., 1978

Tsuji, Masananobu, *Singapore,* Constable &
Co. Ltd, London, England, 1960

Wieneke, James, *Aitape-Wewak Campaign,*
Sidney, Australia, 1962

Record Sources:

Washington National Records Center, GSA,
Suitland, Maryland

Combat History of the U.S. 32nd Infantry Division

Journal, 127th Infantry Regiment - 28 June-25 Aug. 1944

File #735017, Box Group 9249

Hq., 127th Infantry Regiment, APO 32, 30 Aug. 1944 after action reports:

Nor. New Guinea 10 July 1944
Nor. New Guinea 11 July 1944
Nor. New Guinea 12 July 1944
Nor. New Guinea 13 July 1944

Journal, 128th Infantry Regiment - APO 32, 4 May-27 July 1944 after action reports:

Koroko, New Guinea 10 July 1944
Koroko, New Guinea 11 July 1944
Koroko, New Guinea 12 July 1944
Koroko, New Guinea 13 July 1944
Koroko, New Guinea 16 July 1944
Koroko, New Guinea 17 July 1944

Interview Reports:

General Charles Hall, Persecution and Tradewind Task Forces
Lt. Col. Peter Hooper, 112th Cavalry Regiment
Capt. Leonard Lowry, Company I, 127th Regiment, 32nd Division
Lowry Notes: "Action of 3rd Battalion During Aitape Capaign, 1944"

After Action Reports, Alamo Force, Record Group 407

#AE958, 10 May-18 May 1944

#AE1450, 18 May-10 June 1944
#AE1059, 30 June-3 July 1944
#AE 1339, 10 July-11 Aug 1944

PFC-3 112th Cavalry Operations, 8 June-11 July 1944
PFC F1-3, TED Force Operations, 13 July-30 July 1944

USSBS (Atis Reports) of Japanese Sources
    18th Army Operations II, pp 77-80
    18th Army Operations III, pp. 100-206
ORB AGO Collections:
    Operational Order #5- MO Operation against Aitape
    2nd Battalion, 80th Infantry Field Diary, 13 May-14 July 1944
    MO Operation Order #38, 6 July-Aug 31 1944
    43d Infantry Operations Report - Aitape
    Tadji Defense Perimeter Report - 16 June-25 Aug 1944

Albert F. Simpson Historical Research Center, USAF, Maxwell Field, Ala.
    5th Air Force ADVON monthly summaries from March thru August 1944
    Reel #BOO43 - History of the 3rd Bomb Group

Photos: All photos from National Archives and U.S. Air Force

Maps: All maps from U.S. Army Map Service, Washington, DC

SPECIAL NOTE: The author would like thank Mr. Fred Purnell and Mrs. Victoria S. Washington of the Washington National Records Center for their help in researching record information for this book:

Participants:

AMERICAN:

Gen. Douglas MacArthur - Cinc, Southwest Pacific Allied Forces

Gen. George Kenney - CinC, U.S. 5th Air Force

Gen. Charles Hall - commander, Persecution Force, Aitape

Gen. William Gill, commander 32nd Infantry Division

    Col. Robert Fowler, CO, 128th Infantry Regiment

        Lt. Col. Henry Geebs, 2nd Battalion

    Col. Merle Howe, CO - 127th Infantry Regiment

        Lt. Col. Ed Bloch, 3rd Battalion

        Capt. Leonard Lowry, Lowry Force

    Lt. Col. Peter Hooper, 112th Cavalry Regiment

    Maj. William Lewis, 129th Field Artillery

    Capt. William Dale, 114th Combat Engineers

5th Air Force

Lt. Col. Richard Ellis, 3rd Bomb Group
Lt. Col. Charles MacDonald, 475th Eighter Group
Maj. Harry Brown, 9th Fighter Squadron, 49th Fighter Group

JAPANESE:
Gen. Korechiko Anami, CinC, 2nd Area Forces
Gen. Hatazo Adachi, CinC, 18th Army
Gen. Kunachi Teramoto, 4th Air Army
Gen. Sadahiko Miyake, commander, Aitape Assault Force
　Col. Tokutaro Ide, CO, 80th Infantry Regiment
　　Lt. Col. Masanasobu Tsuji, 2nd Battalion
Col. Mitsujiro Matsumoto, CO, 78th Infantry Regiment
Col. Masahuko Nara, CO, 237th Infantry Regiment (Coastal Force)
　Maj. Tadi Yamashita, 1st Battalion
　Maj. Iwataro Hoshimo, CO, 41st Mountain Artillery Battalion

6th Air Division - Gen. Giichi Itabana
　248th Flying Regiment - Capt. Sadaaki Akamatsu
　8th Flying Regiment - Capt. Goro Furugori

THE CONTINUING BOLT SERIES
BY CORT MARTIN

THE GUNN SERIES BY JORY SHERMAN

GUNN #1: DAWN OF REVENGE   (594, $1.95)

Accused of killing his wife, William Gunnison changes his name to Gunn and begins his fight for revenge. He'll kill, maim, turn the west blood red—until he finds the men who murdered his wife.

GUNN #2: MEXICAN SHOWDOWN   (628, $1.95)

When Gunn rode into the town of Cuchillo, he didn't know the rules. But when he walked into Paula's Cantina, he knew he'd learn them.

GUNN #3: DEATH'S HEAD TRAIL   (648, $1.95)

With his hands on his holster and his eyes on the sumptuous Angela Larkin, Gunn goes off hot—on his enemy's trail.

GUNN #4: BLOOD JUSTICE   (670, $1.95)

Gunn is enticed into playing a round with a ruthless gambling scoundrel—and playing around with the scoundrel's estranged wife!

GUNN #8: APACHE ARROWS   (791, $2.25)

Gunn gets more than he bargained for when he rides in with pistols cocked to save a beautiful settler woman from ruthless Apache renegades.

GUNN #9: BOOTHILL BOUNTY   (830, $2.25)

When Gunn receives a desperate plea for help from the sumptuous Trilla, he's quick to respond—because he knows she'll make it worth his while!

GUNN #10: HARD BULLETS   (896, $2.25)

The disappearance of a gunsmith and a wagon full of ammo sparks suspicion in the gunsmith's daughter. She thinks Gunn was involved, and she's up-in-arms!

GUNN #11: TRIAL BY SIXGUN   (918, $2.25)

Gunn offers help to a pistol-whipped gambler and his well-endowed daughter—only to find that he'll have to lay more on the table than his cards!

GUNN #12: THE WIDOW-MAKER   (987, $2.25)

Gunn offers to help the lovely ladies of Luna Creek when the ruthless Widow-maker gang kills off their husbands. It's hard work, but the rewards are mounting!

Available wherever paperbacks are sold, or order direct from the Publisher. Send cover price plus 50¢ per copy for mailing and handling to Zebra Books, 475 Park Avenue South, New York, N.Y. 10016. DO NOT SEND CASH.